P9-DNN-403

THE

RULES OF
WORK

A Definitive Code for
Personal Success

EXPANDED EDITION

RICHARD TEMPLAR

Vice President, Publisher: Tim Moore
Associate Publisher and Director of Marketing: Amy Neidlinger
Operations Manager: Gina Kanouse
Senior Marketing Manager: Julie Phifer
Publicity Manager: Laura Czaja
Assistant Marketing Manager: Megan Colvin
Cover Designer: Sandra Schroeder
Managing Editor: Kristy Hart
Senior Project Editor: Lori Lyons
Proofreader: Gill Editorial Services
Senior Compositor: Gloria Schurick
Manufacturing Buyer: Dan Uhrig

© 2010 by Pearson Education, Inc.

Publishing as FT Press

Upper Saddle River, New Jersey 07458

Authorized adaptation from the original UK edition, entitled *The Rules of Work*, Second Edition, by Richard Templar, published by Pearson Education Limited, © Pearson Education 2010.

This U.S. adaptation is published by Pearson Education Inc, © 2010 by arrangement with Pearson Education Ltd, United Kingdom.

FT Press offers excellent discounts on this book when ordered in quantity for bulk purchases or special sales. For more information, please contact U.S. Corporate and Government Sales, 1-800-382-3419, corpsales@pearsontechgroup.com. For sales outside the U.S., please contact International Sales at international@pearson.com.

Company and product names mentioned herein are the trademarks or registered trademarks of their respective owners.

All rights reserved. No part of this book may be reproduced, in any form or by any means, without permission in writing from the publisher.

Rights are restricted to U.S., its dependencies, and the Philippines.

Printed in the United States of America

First Printing June 2010

ISBN-10: 0-13-707206-6
ISBN-13: 978-0-13-707206-4

Pearson Education LTD.
Pearson Education Australia PTY, Limited.
Pearson Education Singapore, Pte. Ltd.
Pearson Education North Asia, Ltd.
Pearson Education Canada, Ltd.
Pearson Educación de Mexico, S.A. de C.V.
Pearson Education—Japan
Pearson Education Malaysia, Pte. Ltd.

Templar, Richard, 1950-2006.
   The rules of work : a definitive code for personal success / Richard Templar.
      p. cm.
   ISBN-13: 978-0-13-707206-4 (pbk. : alk. paper)
   ISBN-10: 0-13-707206-6
   1. Success in business. 2. Executives. I. Title.
   HF5386.T34 2010
   650.1—dc22
                                    2010001942

Contents

Dedication

I am indebted to Rachael Stock, without whose support, encouragement, and enthusiasm this book would never have happened.

Acknowledgments

I would like to thank all the readers who have emailed me over the years with comments on my books, and especially those who have contributed ideas to this new edition of *The Rules of Work*. In particular, may I thank:

Anil Baddela

Johnson Maganja Grace

David Grigor

Frank Hull

Hubert Rau

Pawan Singh

Tina Steel

Foreword

Most of us (I'm guessing here) want to do our jobs well. Most of us (still guessing) want more important jobs, bigger salaries, greater security, higher status, and a bright future. So we try to do our jobs so well that we will be rewarded, respected, and promoted.

And that is where we go wrong. (I'm not guessing anymore.)

Of course, we have to do our jobs really well. There's no future for the screw-up, the bum, or the sociopath. But Richard Templar puts his finger on the flaw in the implied logic that concludes that the better we do our job, the faster we will rise up the organization. He points out that we are all doing two jobs, but most of us are only conscious of one of them—the job in hand: meeting our sales targets, reducing machine downtime, speeding up monthly management accounts, whatever. The other job is both larger and vaguer: making the organization work. If people think you have it in you to solve the problems of the organization itself, not just your small part of it, you've broken away from the pack. But how do you do that? There's an easy answer: read this book. Follow the Rules.

I realized when I read this book that I have always been half conscious of the Rules, though I never managed to formulate and analyze them with the clarity and detail that Richard Templar brings to the task. There was a time when I had to interview a lot of promotion candidates in the BBC, and with most of them I had this feeling that somehow they didn't look like top management material. Was it how they dressed, how they walked, how they talked? Bits of all of those, but most of all their attitude, their frame of mind, which somehow affected all the others.

Most of them stressed how well they did their present job, which was quite unnecessary. We knew that; that's why they were there. It was their entrance ticket to the interview, and there was no point in constantly waving it at us. Amazingly few of them had given any real thought to the problems of the job they were applying for, as opposed to the job they were doing, let alone the problems that faced the BBC as an organization. They were oblivious of the Rules.

The American management guru Peter Drucker makes a useful distinction between efficiency and effectiveness: efficiency is doing the job right, effectiveness is doing the right job. Your boss will tell you how to do the job right, but you have to work out for yourself what the right job is. It means looking at the world outside the organization: what it needs, and how its needs are changing, and what the organization must do (and stop doing) to survive and prosper.

I remember interviewing two chief executives of great corporations. Both had joined from college with hundreds of other bright ambitious graduates, and I asked them why it was they had gotten to the top of the heap and not any of the others. One said he didn't know, but what he could tell me was that every job he'd ever done was abolished after he left it. The other didn't know either, but said that no job he'd ever done existed until he started doing it. Both of them were striking examples of people who focused on doing the right job, of thinking like the chairman even when they were junior or middle managers. And I have no doubt they followed all the other rules as well, always somehow looking and sounding like someone who should be in a higher job. And as Richard Templar stresses—they were popular and respected throughout the organization. You can't be a successful chief executive if you're surrounded by embittered, resentful, and demoralized colleagues.

The Rules of Work is first and foremost a guide for the individual manager, an eye-opener for all those who would like to rise to the top but don't seem to be able to find the map. But it is also very much a book for the organization itself; the great danger is fossilization, becoming preoccupied with its internal tasks and systems and procedures, and losing touch with the world outside. And this will happen if everyone is concentrating on being efficient rather than being effective—in other words, if they don't follow the Rules.

Sir Antony Jay
Author, *Yes Minister* and creator of Sir Humphrey
Founder, Video Arts

Introduction

I first started formulating *The Rules of Work* many, many years ago when I was an assistant manager. There was a promotion going for the next step up—manager. There were two possible candidates, myself and Rob. On paper I had more experience, more expertise, most of the staff wanted me as their manager, and I generally knew the new job better. Rob, to be honest, was useless.

I was chatting with an outside consultant the company used and asked him what he thought my chances were. "Slim," he replied. I was indignant. I explained all about my experience, my expertise, my superior abilities. "Yep," he replied, "but you don't walk like a manager." "And Rob does?" "Yep, that's about the strength of it." Needless to say he was quite right, and Rob got the job. I had to work under a moron. But a moron who walked right. I studied that walk very carefully.

The consultant was spot on—there was a manager's walk. I began to notice that every employee, every job, everyone in fact, had their walk. Receptionists walked in a particular way, as did the cashiers, the catering staff, the office workers, the admin, the security staff—and the managers, of course. Secretly, I began to practice the walk.

Looking the Part

As I spent a lot of time watching the walk, I realized that there was also a manager's style of attire, of speaking, of behavior. It wasn't enough that I was good at my job and had the experience. I had to *look* as if I was better than anyone else. It wasn't just a walk—it was an entire makeover. And gradually, as I watched, I noticed that what newspaper was read was important, as was what pen was used, how you wrote, how you talked to colleagues, what you said at meetings—everything, in fact, was being judged, evaluated, acted upon. It wasn't enough to be able to do the job. If you wanted to get on, you had to be seen to be the Right Type. *The Rules of Work* is about creating that type—of course, you've got to be able to do the job in the first place. But a lot of people can do that. What makes you stand out? What makes you a suitable candidate for promotion? What makes the difference?

Act One Step Ahead

I noticed that among the managers there were some who had mastered the walk, but there were others who were practicing, unconsciously, for the next walk—the general manager's walk.

I happened at that time to be travelling around a lot between different branches and noticed that among the general managers there were some who were going to stay right where they were for a long time. But there were others already practicing for their next step ahead—the regional director's walk. And style and image.

I switched from practicing the manager's walk and leapt ahead to the general manager's walk. Three months later I was promoted from assistant manager to general manager in one swift move. I was now the moron's manager.

Walk Your Talk

Rob had the walk (*Rule 18: Develop a Style That Gets You Noticed*), but unfortunately he didn't adhere sufficiently to the number one rule—he didn't know the job well enough. He looked right, sounded right, but the bottom line was—he couldn't do the job as well as he should have done. I was brought in over his head because they couldn't sack him—having just promoted him it would have looked bad—and they needed someone to oversee his work so that his errors could be rectified quickly. Rob had reached the level of his own incompetence and stayed there for several years neither improving nor particularly getting worse—just looking good and walking right. He eventually shuffled himself off sideways into running his own business—a restaurant. This failed shortly afterward because he forgot *Rule 2: Never Stand Still*—or maybe he never actually knew it. He carried on walking like a manager instead of a restaurateur. His customers never really took to him.

By practicing the general manager's walk, I got the promotion, but I also got it because I paid great attention to doing my job well—Rule 1. Once in this new job I was, of course, completely out of my depth. I had to quickly learn not only my new role and all its responsibilities, but also the position below, which I had not really held. I had stood in for managers but I had never been a manager—now I was the manager's manager. I was in great danger of falling flat on my face.

Never Let Anyone Know How Hard You Work

But I was, by now, a dedicated Rules Player. There was only one recourse—secret learning. I spent every spare second available—evenings, weekends, lunch breaks—studying everything I could that would help me. But I told no one—*Rule 13*.

Within a short time I had mastered enough to be able to do the job well enough. And the embryonic *Rules of Work* were born.

Have a Plan

Being a general manager was both fun and pain. It was 50 percent more work but only 20 percent more pay. My next step, logically, was regional director. But it didn't appeal. More work—much more work but for not that much more money. I began to develop a plan (*Rules 24–34*). Where did I want to go next? What did I want to do? I was getting bored being stuck in the office all the time and all those endless dreary meetings. And all that time spent at head office. Not for me. I wanted to have fun again. I wanted to practice the Rules. I formulated my plan.

What the company didn't have was a roving troubleshooter—a sort of general manager's general manager. I put *Rule 4: Carve Out a Niche for Yourself* into play. I suggested to the chairman that a report was needed. I never suggested that this was the job I wanted, but the agenda was obvious, I suppose. I got it, of course, and became a peripatetic general manager, answerable directly only to the chairman and with a job description I wrote myself. And pay? A lot more than the regional directors were on, but they didn't know and I didn't let on (*Part V: Look After Yourself*). I cultivated their support and friendship; I was never a threat because it was obvious I wasn't after their job. They may have wanted the money I was making if they had known, but they didn't want the little niche I had carved out for myself.

And I did this without being ruthless, dishonest, or unpleasant. In fact, I was always diplomatic when dealing with the general managers. I treated them with courtesy and politeness, even when I had to confront them on some aspect of their job. I added *If you can't say anything nice—shut up* and learned the rules in *Part VIII: Cultivate Diplomacy*.

Knowing the People Who Count

And I quickly learned that if I wanted to know what was going on in a branch, it was best to speak to the people who really knew—the maintenence staff, the receptionists, the cashiers, the elevator attendant, and the drivers. It was important both to identify these people and to be on the right side of them—*Rule 94*. They supplied me with more information than anyone would have believed—and all for the price of a simple "Hello Bob, how's your daughter doing at college these days?"

The Rules of Work took shape. Over the next few years I watched them grow up and gain maturity and experience. I left the corporation and founded my own consultancy. I trained managers in *The Rules of Work* and watched them go out into the world and conquer their destiny with charm and courtesy, confidence and authority.

But I see you have questions. How do these Rules work—are they manipulative? No, you don't make anyone else do anything; it is you that is changing and improving.

- Do I have to become someone else? No, you may need to change your behavior a bit, but not your personality or values. You'll go on being you, but a slicker, quicker you, a more successful you.

- Are they hard to learn? No, you can learn them in a week or two—but it does take a long time to really master them. But we are learning all the time and even practicing one Rule is better than none at all.

- Is it easy to spot others doing them? Yes, sometimes, but the really good Rules Players will never let you see what they are doing; they're too good for that. But once you become a Rules Player too, it does become easier to see what Rule people are using at any particular time.

- Will I notice benefits right away? Oh yes, you betcha—immediately.

- Do I still do them? I wouldn't even admit to doing them in the first place—I'm a Rules Player after all.

- Is it ethical to use the Rules? Yes. You aren't doing anything wrong, merely utilizing your own natural skills and talents and adapting them, using them consciously. This is a key area for understanding the Rules—consciously. Everything you do will have been decided beforehand—you'll still appear spontaneous, of course, you decided that as well—but you will be a conscious controller of any situation rather than an unconscious victim. You will be awake and aware, living in the moment and taking advantage of your own abilities. The bottom line is that you must be able to do your job—and do it well in the first place. The Rules are not for slackers. You think you work hard now? It's nothing to doing the Rules successfully—now that really does take work.

And let's face it, you love to work. You love doing your job. You have to, to be wanting to read the Rules and to want to be moving up. What I am suggesting is that you consciously think about every area of that work and make changes to improve

- The way you do it

- How people perceive you to be doing it

If you don't practice the Rules, you will muddle along, get by, maybe find what it is you are looking for. You may already know a lot of these Rules—and be practicing them—instinctively and intuitively. Now we will do them consciously. If you do you will

- Get promoted

- Get along better with your colleagues

- Feel better about yourself
- Enjoy your work more
- Understand your job better
- Understand your boss's point of view better
- Take more pride in both yourself and your work
- Set a good example for junior staff
- Contribute more to your company
- Be valued and respected
- Spread an aura of goodwill and cooperation around you
- Be successful if you leave to start your own business.

These Rules are simple and effective, safe and practical. They are your 10 steps to building confidence and creating a new and more powerful you. And building that new you morally and ethically. You aren't going to do anything that you wouldn't expect—and appreciate—others doing to you. These Rules enhance personal standards and elevate your individual principles. They are my gift to you. They're yours. Keep them safe, keep them secret.

PART I

WALK YOUR TALK

These first Rules are the underlying ones that govern all the others—know your job well, do it well, and be better than anyone else at doing it. It's that simple. The secret part is to make sure nobody knows how hard you have to work to do it so well. You can do all your learning in secret, in private—don't let on, and don't let anyone know you do this—and never ever let anyone know you've read this book; it is your secret bible. The important thing is to look calm and efficient, on top of everything and totally in control. You glide through your daily work with ease and confidence. You are unflappable and unstoppable. Bottom line is, however, you must be really good at your basic job.

RULE 1

Get Your Work Noticed

It's all too easy for your work to get overlooked in the busy hurly-burly of office life. You're slaving away, and it can be hard to remember that you need to put in some effort to boost your individual status and personal kudos for your work. But it's important. You have to make your mark so you stand out and your promotional potential will be realized.

The best way to do this is to step outside the normal working routine. If you have to process so many widgets each day—and so does everyone else—then processing more won't do you that much good. But if you submit a report to your boss of how everyone could process more widgets, then you'll get noticed. The unsolicited report is a brilliant way to stand out from the crowd. It shows you're thinking on your feet and using your initiative. But it mustn't be used too often. If you subject your boss to a barrage of unsolicited reports, you'll get noticed but in completely the wrong way. You have to stick to certain Rules:

- Only submit a report occasionally.
- Make really sure that your report will actually work—that it will do good or provide benefits.
- Make sure your name is prominently displayed.
- Make sure the report will be seen not only by your boss, but by his boss as well.
- It doesn't have to be a report—it can be an article in the company newsletter.

Of course, the very best way to get your work noticed is to be very, very good at your job. And the best way to be good at your job is to be totally dedicated to doing the job and ignoring all the rest. There is a vast amount of politics, gossip, gamesmanship, time wasting, and socializing that goes on in the name of work. It isn't work. Keep your eye on the ball, and you'll already be playing with a vast advantage over your colleagues. The Rules Player stays focused. Keep your mind on the task at hand—being very good at your job—and don't get distracted.

> **THE UNSOLICITED REPORT IS A BRILLIANT WAY TO STAND OUT FROM THE CROWD.**

RULE 2

Never Stand Still

Most people go into work each day with only one thought—getting through to going home time. During their day they will do whatever they have to, to arrive at that magic time. You won't. You won't stand still. Having gotten the job seems enough for most people that they will just do it and thus remain static. But doing the job isn't the end game for you—it is merely a means to the end. And the end for you is promotion, more money, success, amassing the contacts and experience to set out on your own, whatever it is that is on your wish list. The job, in a way, is an irrelevance.

Yes, you have to do the work. And yes, you have to do it supremely well. But your eye should already be on the next step, and every activity you indulge in at work should be merely a step in your plan to move up.

While others are thinking of their next coffee break or how to get through the afternoon without actually having to do any work, you will be busy planning and executing your next maneuver. In an ideal world, the Rules Players will have gotten their work done by lunchtime so that they have the afternoon free to study for the next promotion, to assess the competition among close colleagues, to write the unsolicited reports to get their work noticed, to research ways to improve the work process for everyone, to further their knowledge of company procedures and history.

If you can't get your work done by lunchtime, then you will have to fit all these things into and around the work. What the competition will be doing is not doing them. But you don't stand still. Never accept that doing the job is enough. That's for the others. You will be moving right along preparing, studying, analyzing, and learning.

We talked earlier about the manager's walk; well, that's what you'll be doing, practicing the manager's walk—or whoever's walk it is you need to master. You have to see promotion—or whatever else it is you want—as a movement. You keep moving or you grow moss. You have to have movement or you grow stagnant. You have to like movement or you grow roots.

Movement requires of you that you don't sit on your backside and do nothing—don't stand still.

> IN AN IDEAL WORLD, THE RULES PLAYERS WILL HAVE GOTTEN THEIR WORK DONE BY LUNCHTIME SO THAT THEY HAVE THE AFTERNOON FREE.

RULE 3

Volunteer Carefully

A lot of people think that if they say "yes" to everything, they will get noticed, get praised, and get promoted. Not true. The clever manager above them will use this "I'll do it" mentality, and you will end up overworked, undervalued, and abused. Before you put your hand up to volunteer for anything, think very carefully. You have to ask yourself various questions:

- Why is this person asking for volunteers?
- How will this further my plan?
- How will I look to senior management if I volunteer?
- How will I look if I don't volunteer?
- Is this a dirty job that no one else wants?
- Or is this person genuinely, desperately overburdened and really in need of my help?

It might well be a dirty job that no one else wants, and by volunteering you might look very good in the eyes of senior management—they think you capable of rising to a challenge, being useful, and being prepared to get your sleeves rolled up and stuck in. On the other hand, they might think you are an idiot. Or if you volunteer to do the filing, they'll see you as a mere filing clerk. Or you might generate a load of goodwill for helping out someone in real need of support. Be careful and choose your moments. There's no point sticking your hand up if it means you're going to be seen as a monkey. Only take that one step forward when you are confident you will look good, gain benefit, or make a difference to someone who needs help.

Also be aware that sometimes you seem to have volunteered without putting your hand up or stepping forward. It just happens that sometimes all your colleagues take a collective step backward, leaving you there out in the open seemingly volunteering when you really had no intention of doing so. The first time this happens, you will have to ride with it and do the job—but make sure it doesn't happen again—not to a Rules Player, not twice. Keep your ear better attuned next time and feel out the collective approach. Make sure you're stepping backward with the rest of them.

> BEFORE YOU PUT YOUR
> HAND UP TO VOLUNTEER
> FOR ANYTHING, THINK
> VERY CAREFULLY.

Carve Out a Niche for Yourself

I once worked with a colleague who made it a great personal skill to find out stuff about customers that we couldn't. It seemed he always knew the names of their children, where they went on vacation, their birthdays—and their spouses'— their favorite music and restaurants. Consequently, if you had to deal with a particular customer you went to Mike and asked, politely and humbly, if he could give you some little titbit that would get you well in with the customer. Mike had carved out a niche for himself. No one asked him to become a walking encyclopedia of customer likes and dislikes. It wasn't part of his job description. It took a lot of work and unseen effort. And it was a very valuable asset. It didn't take long for the regional director to hear of this extra effort Mike had put in, and his rise up the corporate ladder was swift, meteoric, unprecedented. That's all it took. I say "all," but it was in fact a lot of work and immensely clever.

Carving out a niche means spotting a useful area that no one else has spotted. It might be as simple as being great at spreadsheets or report writing. It might be, like Mike, knowing something no one else does. It might be being brilliant with company software or budgets or understanding the system. Make sure you don't make yourself indispensable, or this rule backfires.

Carving out a niche for yourself often takes you out of the normal range of office activities. You get to move around more, be out of the office more often without having to explain to anyone where you are or what you are doing. This makes you stand out from the herd and gives you independence and a superior quality. I once volunteered to edit the company newsletter—bearing in mind the previous rule—and could wander about between our seven branches at will. Obviously, I always made sure my work was done on time and supremely well.

Carving out a niche for yourself frequently means you get noticed by people other than your boss—other people's bosses. These bosses get together and they talk. If they bring your name up it will be in a good way—"I see Rich has been busy doing some really original market analysis." This makes it difficult for your boss not to promote you if she wants to win her peer group approval. If the other bosses think you are a good idea, then your boss really has to go along with it.

> IF THE OTHER BOSSES THINK YOU ARE A GOOD IDEA, THEN YOUR BOSS REALLY HAS TO GO ALONG WITH IT.

RULE 5

Under Promise and Over Deliver

If you know you can do it by Wednesday, always say Friday. If you know it will take your department a week, say two. If you know it will cost an extra two people to get the new machine installed and up and running, then say three.

This isn't dishonest, merely prudent. If it gets spotted that this is what you do, then openly and honestly admit it and say you always build a contingency percentage into your calculations. They can't kill you for that.

That's the first bit. Under promise. And just because you have said Friday or two weeks or whatever doesn't mean you can coast and use up that allowance. Oh, no. What you have to do is make sure you deliver early, on budget, and better than promised. And that's the second part. Over deliver. This means if you promised to have the report finished by Monday first thing, it is finished, but not only is it a report it also contains the full implementation plans for the new premises. Or if you said you'd have the exhibition stand up and running by Sunday night with only two extra members of staff, you have—and you've managed to get your major competitor to pull out of the show. Or if you said you'd have a rough proposal written for the new company brochure by the next meeting, you not only have this but also a full color mock-up, the complete text written and proofread, all the photos taken, and full printing costs and quotes for distribution. Obviously, you've got to be careful that you don't overstep the mark and assume responsibilities you haven't been given, but I'm sure you get the idea.

RULE 5

Again, it might be stating the obvious, but don't be too blatant when you do this or your boss will get to expect it—it should be a pleasant surprise, not a frequently used tactic.

It also helps sometimes to act dumb. You can pretend you don't really understand some new technique or software when in reality you know it back to front. Then when you suddenly do all the budgets on the spreadsheets that no one else could, you look good. If, in advance, you had said "Oh, yes, I know that, I worked with these spreadsheets at my last place," there is no surprise, and you've given the game away—and your advantage.

When you under promise and over deliver, you have to have a bottom line—in your case, as a Rules Player, it is simply that you will *never* deliver late or deliver short. That's it. If you have to sweat blood and work all night, then so be it. You will deliver when you said you would—or earlier if you can—without exception. It is better to negotiate a longer delivery time in the first place than to have to let someone down. A lot of people are so keen to be liked, or approved of, or praised that they will agree to the first delivery time offered to them—"Oh yes, I can do that," and then they fail. They look like pushovers in the first place and incompetent in the last.

> YOU WILL *NEVER* DELIVER
> LATE OR DELIVER SHORT.

RULE 6

Learn to Ask Why

You won't be able to do your best for your employer if you can't see the big picture. You may be only a humble cog in a huge grinding machine, but if you can't step back and see what the whole machine is up to, you won't be able to do your little coggy things as well as you could. What's more, if you only ever talk in terms of your cog and your immediate neighboring cogs and bolts and shafts and pistons, everyone around you will see you as belonging neatly in that little part of the machine.

But you have aspirations to move into bigger and more important parts of the machine, don't you? Of course you do—you're a Rules Player. You want to grow and develop and make a bigger contribution. And to do that—and be seen as a suitable candidate to do that—you need to understand what drives the whole thing and what its purpose is.

The way you do that is to ask questions. When your boss briefs on any new task or project, ask how it fits into the big picture. Why are you shifting focus to selling by phone? Is this a standard market trend, or is your company trying to do something innovative? Why is the accounts department splitting into two—is this to benefit customers or to help the internal structure? And so on.

I'm not talking about plaguing your boss with questions about what color paper clip you should use for the pink triplicate sheets and whether it's OK to put your vacation request in via email. I'm talking about taking an interest in the whole organization and not just your corner of it, and letting your boss see that you have your eye on the big picture.

RULE 6

One of the reasons for this is, of course, that your boss will start to see you as someone who is capable of working at a higher level with a bigger overview, and someone who has a loyalty and concern for the whole company. But you'll also find that your own job makes far more sense when you can see the wider view, and that you're more motivated when you understand the reasons behind changes, new directives, extra work, or special projects.

> I'M TALKING ABOUT
> TAKING AN INTEREST IN
> THE WHOLE ORGANIZATION
> AND NOT JUST YOUR
> CORNER OF IT.

RULE 7

Be 100 Percent Committed

Being a Rules Player means you are going to have to work a whole lot harder than any of your colleagues. They can coast; you can't. They can afford to lighten up and put their feet up; you can't. To move up, you have to be 100 percent committed. You can't afford to lose sight of your long-term goal for a second. For you there is no time off, no downtime, no lounging around time, no slipups, no mistakes, no accidental deviations from the script.

You have to become like a master criminal—they lead incredibly law-abiding lives because they can't risk breaking a tiny law in case it draws attention to themselves and the really big crimes get revealed—and watch what you say and what you do.

If any of this seems too much, then bow out now. I only want committed Rules Players on this team. You are going to have to sign an oath in blood if you want to make this grade. You are going to have to be vigilant, dedicated, watchful, keen, ready, prepared, cautious, alert, and on the ball. Tall order.

Is it worth it? You bet. In the land of the blind, you will be the only one with both eyes open and seeing. You will be powerful—and most importantly you will be having fun. There is no greater buzz than seeing the games that are going on around you and being completely uninvolved, utterly objective, and supremely detached.

You will find that you won't have to do very much once you start observing. You will be able to give people a tiny nudge to get them to change direction rather than a huge big shove. Your dealings will become incredibly delicate and gentle.

But you really do have to be 100 percent committed. If you try this stuff without such dedication, you will go off half-cocked and run the risk of looking foolish instead of cool and in control. But the beauty of total commitment is that you no longer have any decisions to make. You know your path exactly and in any situation you only have to ask, "Does this further my Rule playing or not?"—and then the decision is made for you. Easy.

> YOU ARE GOING TO HAVE TO BE VIGILANT, DEDICATED, WATCHFUL, KEEN, READY, PREPARED, CAUTIOUS, ALERT, AND ON THE BALL.

RULE 8

Learn from Others' Mistakes

A clever man learns from his own mistakes, but a wise man learns from others' mistakes. That's what they say, and any Rules Player with sense follows this principle. We all make some mistakes, but the fewer you make the better.

It sounds good, doesn't it? However, you can't just have the odd catchy quote up your sleeve. You have to really do this stuff. That means that every time someone near you messes up, you need to know all about it. You'll have to do your detective work, subtly mind you. No one wants to be cross-examined by a colleague about where they went wrong, and there's a danger of coming across as smug and self-satisfied and nosy and condescending because it wasn't you who made the mistake, and that is definitely non-Rules behavior.

So when a colleague gets himself in hot water, find out what went wrong without getting spotted. One of the best ways to do this is to offer to help him put things right. After all, this isn't a competition, and we don't actually want our teammates to mess up. It's just that if they do it anyway, we might as well get some benefit from it. Helping them remedy things can be a great way of finding out exactly what happened.

Once you've found out just what went wrong, work out how and why it happened. Then be brutally honest with yourself about whether you could have made the same mistake. Have you ever been in a hurry and failed to double-check the paper-work? Or forgotten to check your voice mail at the end of the day? Or negotiated on the basis of figures you took as right but could actually have been inaccurate? Or written down the wrong delivery date in your diary? If so, you need to devise some kind of system now to make sure it can't happen in the future; otherwise it's only a matter of time before you make the same mistake. And remember, if you've already witnessed your colleague getting it wrong, you'll look even worse when it subsequently happens to you.

Over time, you'll find that a thorough and inquiring attitude to other people's mistakes, rather than a complacent, "It won't happen to me" approach, will more than pay off. And the fewer mistakes you make, the more you'll impress the boss. It's as simple as that.

EVERY TIME SOMEONE
NEAR YOU MESSES UP,
YOU NEED TO KNOW ALL
ABOUT IT.

RULE 9

Enjoy What You Are Doing

If you're not enjoying yourself, what are you doing? If there is no entertainment value in your work, then there really is no point in doing it—you can probably get enough in unemployment benefit to survive. I think there are an awful lot of people out there who really do enjoy working but are frightened to say so in case they get accused of being workaholics or sad or something.

There is no shame in saying you enjoy your work. There seems to be some kudos in being miserable at work, in moaning about your situation. There is a sort of office pecking order where people try to outdo each other in moaning about how much they hate their work.

Not for you there's not. The Rules Player enjoys work and makes sure people know that. Once you acknowledge that work is fun—and for you it is even more fun than for anyone else—you will find your step lightens, your stress levels decrease, and your whole demeanor lightens. By admitting work is fun, you are trading in a secret bit of knowledge that only really successful people usually have. Work is fun—engrave it on your heart.

Having a good time at work and realizing work is good isn't the same thing. Work being good means you take pride in what you do, enjoy the challenge, and look forward to each day with optimism and enthusiasm. Having a good time at work means not achieving much, talking a lot, winding up colleagues, and drinking champagne all afternoon. There is a difference, I'm sure you will agree. Having a good time at work

RULE 9

is a temporary thing. It lasts while the fun lasts but quickly flags once the excitement, the elation, has worn off.

Work being good means enjoying the negotiating, the hiring and firing, the day-to-day challenges, the stresses and disappointments, the uncertain future, the testing of one's mettle, the new learning curves. A surprising number of people die within a year of retirement—this suggests that work is more important to our existence than we think.

If you ain't enjoying all this and appreciating that it is enjoyable, then you are doomed to be one of the moaners, one of life's victims.

> THERE IS NO SHAME IN
> SAYING YOU ENJOY
> YOUR WORK.

Develop the Right Attitude

At work a lot of people have a sort of "us and them" attitude. They like to side with the "workers" and moan about the "management." You, on the other hand, will develop the right attitude and not become one of the "us" mentality. No matter what your position now, you are the next head of department, an embryonic chairman of the board, a budding managing director. You have to start to look at both sides of a situation and identify the position of "them." You may not voice this and may even, in public, appear to side with your fellow workers and colleagues. But deep down, in your heart, you understand and side with "them." Never forget that. Your colleagues may moan about management policy, but you will analyze it and try to see it from their point of view. To fit in and blend you may be tempted to adopt the camouflage of a moaning worker—not a wise move. Nod in agreement, but don't moan yourself.

The right attitude is twofold:

1. You side with management and see policy decision from their point of view.
2. You devote your attention to becoming a total and committed Rules Player—you look out for Number One (that's you).

The right attitude means giving it your best shot, not just today but every day. Not just when it's easy but when it's awful as well.

The right attitude means going that extra mile, giving it that extra effort even when you're tired and pissed off and ready to quit. Others can quit, but you can't. You're a Rules Player.

The right attitude is head up, never moaning, always positive and upbeat, constantly looking for the advantage and the edge.

The right attitude is developing standards—and sticking to them. Being sure of your bottom line and knowing when to make a stand. The right attitude is being aware that you have enormous power and that you will exercise that power with kindness, restraint, humanity, and consideration. You won't put anyone down or be ruthless or manipulative. Yes, you may take advantage of others' sleepiness or apathy or wrong attitude—that's their problem. But you will take the moral high ground and be blameless. The right attitude is being good but quick, kind but observant, considerate but successful.

> YOU WILL TAKE THE
> MORAL HIGH GROUND AND
> BE BLAMELESS.

Be Passionate but Don't Kill Yourself

I hope you're very passionate about your job. Whether your job satisfaction comes from the people you work with, the sense of achievement, a deep belief in what you're doing, the recognition you get, the money you earn, or anything else—I hope you get enough out of the job to feel very passionate about doing it.

But don't fall into the trap of thinking that if you're passionate you have to work long hours and jump through countless hoops to prove it. Being passionate isn't the same thing as staying late at the office. If you have a positive sense of belief in your work and an enthusiasm for it, that will shine through. Your boss will recognize it and, I trust, appreciate it, regardless of the hours you put in.

It isn't necessary to work yourself into the ground to be passionate about your work. In fact, it's hard to sustain your love of a job that is slowly draining all your energy. It's what you achieve that counts, not how long it takes you to achieve it. You might argue that if you're really passionate you should be able to achieve the same as other people in a fraction of the time. OK, that may not mean you can go home by mid-afternoon, but it does mean that your passion will keep your output high even if you knock off at 5:30 like everyone else.

Being passionate about your work, which is generally regarded as being a Good Thing, is about caring whether you do a good job. It's not about how you work; it's about how you feel. So not only do you not have to work long hours to prove your passion, but it wouldn't prove it anyway because it's quite possible to work 16 hours a day and still not care about what you do. It would be a pretty miserable life, granted, but I've known people do it.

So cultivate a positive enthusiasm about your work. If you don't feel passionate about it, look for a new way to view it that makes you care, or work out what would generate that kind of passion in you, and then create it in your work. Now, I'm not saying it's easy. For some people it's a lifelong search. But I'll promise you one thing—if you're not even looking, you'll never find it.

> IT'S NOT ABOUT HOW YOU WORK; IT'S ABOUT HOW YOU FEEL.

RULE 12

Manage Your Energy

Have you heard of time management? Of course you have. Everyone has. I hope you're good at it and doing everything you can to improve. There's always room to manage our time better, and the more effectively you work, the more you will achieve and the more time you'll have left over for yourself as well.

What gets less well promoted is the need to manage your energy. I don't know why this is, since your energy is one of your most essential resources and it doesn't look after itself. You need to bring plenty of energy to what you do at work, and it's your job to make sure that energy is there when it's needed.

In part this means looking after your physical energy. Make sure you stay fit and healthy, and don't wear yourself out when you have work the next day. Just as we make the kids go to bed on time when it's school tomorrow, so you should make sure you don't stay up late, overeat, get drunk, wear yourself out, skip breakfast, or otherwise reduce your potential at work.

And don't forget your mental energy. What time of day do you work best? On a full stomach or just a comfortable one with no hunger pains? What environment makes you most effective at work—quiet, busy, pressured, noisy, companionable? We're all different, and you may not have total control over your working day, but you can make sure those tasks that need concentration get allocated to times when you're best able to concentrate and so on.

RULE 12

And there's emotional energy too. If things are going badly in your home life, you need to find ways to bolster your emotional mood before you get to work in the morning so your job isn't affected (there's more on this in *Rule 14: Keep Your Home Life at Home*). If you're under emotional pressure at work, again, you'll need to come up with constructive ways to keep your energy levels up—go for a run at lunchtime, tackle the person who's bugging you, talk to your boss about your worries.

Finally, your spiritual side needs room to stretch to feel energized. For some people this can happen outside work, while others need to be doing a job that gives them a strong sense of moral worth. Only you know where you stand on this, but make sure that your job isn't cramping your spiritual energy, or in the end both you and the job will suffer.

> IT'S YOUR JOB TO MAKE
> SURE THAT ENERGY IS
> THERE WHEN IT'S NEEDED.

RULE 13

Never Let Anyone Know How Hard You Work

Look at someone like Richard Branson. He's always seen as playing, flying balloons, living on a converted barge, flying to the States. You never see him sitting at a desk, answering phones, doing paperwork. But at some time during his working day that is exactly what he must do. We just don't get to see it. Thus we think of him as the business playboy, the happy-go-lucky entrepreneur, the devilish entertainer. It's a neat image and one that he seems very happy to go along with—and why not?

This is the sort of image the intrepid Rules Player wants to cultivate—suave, easy, relaxed, languid, in control, and very chilled. You never run, never panic, never even seem to hurry. Yes, you may stay up until the early hours of every morning, but you will never admit this. Yes, you may work through your vacations, weekends, and days off, but you will never let on, never moan about how hard you work or the hours you put in. To the outside observer you are coasting, taking it easy, taking it all in your stride.

Obviously, to be able to do this you have to be very good at your job. If you ain't, then you're going to fail trying this Rule out for size. So, what do you do if you aren't very good at your job? Burn that midnight oil again getting good. Learn, study, gain experience and knowledge, read, ask questions, revise, sweat, and cram until you do know that job inside and out. Do this first, and then you can wonder about looking cool and very relaxed.

RULE 13

There are a few Rules within this Rule:

- Never ask for an extension of a deadline.
- Never ask for help: never admit that you are out of your depth—you can ask for guidance, advice, information, an opinion, but never help.
- Never moan or complain about how much work you have to do.
- Learn to be assertive so you don't get overloaded—this is not about letting others know how hard you do work, but you don't have to overdo it and overwork.
- Never be seen breaking into a sweat.
- Always look for ways to ease your workload—unnoticed of course—and ways to speed things up.

> ## TO BE ABLE TO DO THIS YOU HAVE TO BE VERY GOOD AT YOUR JOB.

RULE 14

Keep Your Home Life at Home

When you go to work, you're supposed to be focused on work. To get on with your job. If you spend your time focused on what goes on at home, people will assume you're not really committed to your job. And they'll probably be right, if the truth be told.

Think of the people you've worked with in the past—or indeed now—who spent their time chatting about their families, relating details of their social life, complaining about their mother, fantasizing about their vacations, discussing their latest shopping trip, whining about health care, and telling you about their plans for Christmas. How many of them would you describe as passionate and committed to their work? Probably none of them.

You don't have to keep your personal life so private that your colleagues don't even know that you have kids, that your mother is in the hospital, or that you enjoy fishing. But you do have to keep your personal life well in the background and concentrate on your job during working hours. That will ensure that you do the best job you can in the quickest time and the most effective way. That will ensure that your boss, and your boss's boss, see you as a focused and enthusiastic worker. And that will ensure that you enjoy the job more and find it more satisfying—no one can enjoy themselves fully when their mind is elsewhere.

Your colleagues don't need to know about your personal problems. Sure, you need to have an outlet and good friends to talk to, but not during working hours. If you have good friends among your coworkers, have a drink after work to discuss your problems.

Listen, everyone has an ailing parent, a child who's going through a tricky patch at school, an irritating neighbor, a mortgage they can barely afford, or a sister-in-law from hell coming to stay for the weekend. They don't need to hear about your problems. Sorry, but that's the way it is. I'm not unsympathetic, but this isn't the time or the place for it.

Of course, I realize that there are occasionally major problems that will have some impact on your work. One of those very rare and exceptional events like a divorce or a bereavement. In these cases, of course, you won't be able to hide it at work, and you should let your boss know why you're not quite so on the ball for a few days or weeks. But if you're doing your best, and you have a reputation for being work-focused and keeping your personal life out of the job, the people around you will be so much more understanding and sympathetic when you really need them to be.

> ## NO ONE CAN ENJOY THEMSELVES FULLY WHEN THEIR MIND IS ELSEWHERE.

PART II

KNOW THAT YOU'RE BEING JUDGED AT ALL TIMES

Everything about us speaks volumes to others. The way we dress, the car we drive, where we go on vacation, how we talk and walk, what we eat at lunchtime—everything about us is subject to the judgment of others.

The following Rules are about making sure that the judgment is positive and enhances your career. If you've never thought about it before, these Rules will help you recognize the signals you give off and how to improve them so others take notice. You can't stop people from making judgments—but you can change those judgments and consciously affect them. These Rules are about being stylish, confident, smart, well groomed, and very smooth.

Cultivate a Smile

Remember the poem? "If you can keep your head, etc."—well, how do you let them know you are keeping your head? Easy—smile. Smile no matter what. Smile when you greet your colleagues in the morning. Smile when you shake hands. Smile when it's getting tough. Smile when it's hell. Smile no matter what.

And what sort of smile? Friendly, genuine—make sure it extends to your eyes—sincere, frank, honest, open, happy. And the easiest way to make your smile all these things is to believe them all. This can't be an act or it'll be spotted immediately. It has to be genuine to appear genuine. You have to feel happy. You have to be enjoying this or your smile will look insincere and false. And if you're not enjoying this, then stop pretending with a fake smile and get the hell out.

We'll assume your smile is real and that it comes from genuine happiness and friendliness. Now it is legit to improve on your smile, to rehearse it, to make it better. But it has to be there in the first place. We'll assume it is.

Look in the mirror and smile. Chances are it will look all wrong. Of course it will. You can only see yourself front on. And photos don't work either, they're in 2D and there is a lot missing when you look at them. You need to see your smile from all angles, in 3D, and there is only one way to see this and that is on film—video or whatever.

If you feel embarrassed getting a partner or friend to video you so you can improve your smile, then you'll have to set it up yourself. Please don't make the mistake I once made. I was a finance manager and was asked to cover for one of our super-market managers for an afternoon. The store was empty, and I spent a most enjoyable afternoon practicing my walk, my smile, my general appearance on the CCTV system in the store. I would go back to the office and watch the results as I changed a slight part of whatever bit I was unhappy with. It was great fun. A few weeks later I was invited to watch a special show for all the staff. Yes, I had forgotten to wipe the tape and the shop manager—bless him—had found it and had been putting on shows for all the general staff. I was forced to sit through the whole thing while my coworkers commented on it and pointed out where I was going wrong. Very droll, very funny.

So to improve your smile, make sure you aren't doing a lop-sided grin, that your teeth can be seen but not too much, that you look happy and honest. Keep practicing until you get it right.

> # IT HAS TO BE GENUINE TO APPEAR GENUINE.

No Limp Fish—Develop the Perfect Handshake

We shake hands often and usually quite unconsciously. How many times do you have to shake hands during a normal business week? And how much thought do you give to it? There are so many signals given during that brief handshake though, that you really ought to make it supremely confident, utterly secure, and convincingly reassuring. When someone shakes hands with you, he should be left with the impression of strength, confidence, power, and of someone totally in control of himself—that's you, of course. If you are in any doubt about the "rightness" of your handshake, get a friend to tell you.

How do you make it better? Make it firm. You can always use the other hand to reassuringly grip both your hand and that of your boss/colleague/client. But don't overdo it and leave this person with crushed fingers.

You can always adapt your handshake to make it more individual, more memorable. My grandfather had a wonderful handshake. He just used his first two fingers (the fore and index) and his thumb and gripped very firmly. You felt as if you were shaking hands with royalty.

Handshakes are very formal, old-fashioned things. Forget about the high fives, the Masonic twitches, or anything gangsta-style. Stick to the old-fashioned sort of shake and you will be remembered as someone confident and authoritative.

Good shakers are the ones who proffer their hand first as well as shaking well. They exude confidence by announcing their name and offering their hand at the same time thus showing keenness, friendliness, a relaxed and confident approach, and a general air of assertiveness. They also look you in the eyes and say your name back to you. We like hearing our own name, and it's an aide memoire.

When you do announce your name, the word that goes first is "Hello." That's it. You might like to be modern and friendly and say "Hi"—that's up to you. But the good Rules Player says "Hello." And follows that with her name. And your name is also formal and old fashioned. It is never "Hi, I'm Dave, from Marketing." The effect is pleasant enough and certainly friendly, but you will have impressed no one, gained no benefit or advantage, and brought yourself down to just about the level of the most junior person there. Much better to say, "Hello, I'm David Simpson, Marketing Manager." This immediately separates you from the herd and makes you more senior to anyone else there. Follow this up with a firm, confident handshake, and you will have them eating out of your hand.

> FORGET ABOUT THE HIGH FIVES, THE MASONIC TWITCHES, OR ANYTHING GANGSTA-STYLE.

RULE 17

Exude Confidence and Energy

I once had to give a talk to a large group of businesswomen about stress management. As I walked to the front to start my talk, I noticed that there was no lectern for notes (not that I had any anyway), nowhere to stand. There was a desk with a chair behind it. If I sat there I would have been lost to view to anyone who wasn't in the front row, and it would have seemed very stilted and formal. I could have stood there with my arms behind my back looking like Prince Charles talking to the palace staff. I could have stood there with my hands by my side or clasped in front of my groin like an embarrassed schoolboy. But I was about to talk about stress—and its management. I needed to look relaxed, calm—as if I was practicing what I was preaching, walking my talk.

I solved my dilemma by sitting on the edge of the desk. I could swing my legs, lean back, lean forward, almost lie down if I wanted. I met someone several years later who had been there and she said that she couldn't remember a thing I'd said but had been impressed by how relaxed I'd seemed—and how when I'd finished talking I sprang up and went off for photos with the local journalist. I don't remember that bit, but she said I seemed confident, relaxed, but also energetic.

That's what we're aiming for. When you walk through the office first thing in the morning, there should be a spring to your step. Let the others crawl in looking hung over or freshly risen from bed or exhausted from long hours commuting. You will arrive fresh and energetic, ready for the day's work, which is easy to deal with, a mere nothing. Walk quickly rather than slowly—quick means keen, means energy, means awake and lively and ready for the challenges the day will throw your way.

Not too quick though, or you'll seem to be in a rush. You need to be smoothly in control—not hurried, not sluggardly, not cowed or beaten. You need to be seen as bright and fresh and alive and enthusiastic.

> WHEN YOU WALK THROUGH THE OFFICE FIRST THING IN THE MORNING, THERE SHOULD BE A SPRING TO YOUR STEP.

RULE 18

Develop a Style That Gets You Noticed

The word is "style." That means tasteful, formal, civilized, sophisticated, elegant, cultured, refined, and discerning. You are going to develop a style that gets you noticed in all these things. Dying your hair red and only ever wearing Goodwill clothes may indeed be a style and one that does get you noticed, but it's not for the Rules Player. Think Cary Grant rather than Boy George. Think Lauren Bacall rather than Madonna. All have style, all attracted attention. But trust me, Cary or Lauren is what you want. Classic, timeless, quality. You have various options if you want to adopt a style:

- Choose one thing and get known for it—always wear black, or double breasted, or Armani, or have a classy handbag/briefcase collection. Develop a trademark dress style—and stick to it.

- Only ever buy the very best you can afford.

- Never wear anything tight—loose clothes talk of quality and elegance, tight clothes of poverty and cheapness.

- Less is more—cut down on jewelry and buy/wear only the very best, the finest. If it's not expensive, then don't wear it. You'll find that if you only limit yourself to very expensive items, it helps you eliminate anything that might be considered dubious or of questionable taste—spending a lot makes you much more discriminating.

- If you wear make-up, then stick to what suits you, what makes you look good. Don't change your makeup with the seasons or with what's in vogue—be known for your look, be instantly recognizable, be stylish.

Always dress up rather than down—formal is best, informal is worst.

Make sure all accessories follow the same Rules as your dress sense—stylish, expensive, loose, recognizable, tasteful. There's not a lot of point in looking good and then dragging round a battered old briefcase that's seen better days—not unless, of course, that's your trademark, in which case make sure the briefcase is very old and very battered and very expensive.

> THINK CARY GRANT
> RATHER THAN
> BOY GEORGE.
> THINK LAUREN BACALL
> RATHER THAN MADONNA.

Pay Attention to Personal Grooming

Each and every morning you need to check that your personal grooming is in tip-top condition. Details really matter. You let one thing go and it will be noticed—and it could be the one thing that makes the vital difference between a promotion and a rejection. Make each day as conscientious as an interview day. Before you leave for work check:

- Shoes shined and in good repair.
- Clothes pressed, clean, new, in good condition—no buttons off, no rips, tears, or splits.
- You are freshly showered, deodorant in place.
- Hair clean every day—and well cut and styled on a regular and consistent basis.
- Men shaved—if you have to have facial hair, check for straggly hairs, insects, fluff, or mold.
- Women made up—this can be as simple as you want, but it must be good, consistent, and perfect.
- Teeth clean and in good repair, breath fresh, tongue clean (no yellow fur).
- Nails clean and freshly manicured.
- Hands clean and no ingrained grime from working on old cars or DIY or gardening—wear thin surgical gloves for all those dirty jobs.
- If you smoke/drink a lot of coffee, make sure your teeth (or hands for smokers) aren't stained, and use mints/chewing gum to avoid dog breath.

- Nose (and ear) hair tidied up/removed.
- If you wear glasses, make sure they suit you, are renewed on a yearly basis so that you can see, are a perfect fit, and are in good condition—no cracked lenses or tape repairs.

You don't have to become vain or to keep checking yourself in the mirror. Once you have got it right, relax and enjoy it. I worked with a woman who would go and clean her teeth after every coffee or sticky bun. Nothing wrong with that except it drew attention to herself and her colleagues thought her strange and obsessive. Her fault was not in cleaning her teeth so often but in making such a song and dance out of it. A little discretion would have been much better.

> ## MAKE EACH DAY AS CONSCIENTIOUS AS AN INTERVIEW DAY.

RULE 20

Be Attractive

There is no doubt about it, and statistics back it up: handsome people get on better than those less fortunate in this regard. Handsome people have to work less hard to get ahead. But what makes someone attractive, handsome? If you look at someone you consider attractive, you will be hard pressed to see what it is they've got that makes them so good looking. Attractiveness, if we ignore the obvious physical impairments such as buck teeth or a warty nose—all of which can be corrected—is very hard to define. Take any Hollywood stars, such as Liza Minelli, Woody Allen, Julia Roberts, and Sean Penn, who aren't classically good looking, and we can see that they have charisma, charm, magnetism, a larger-than-life attitude. They come right out at you. They have life, presence, drama, power, and personality.

You too must have these things. They are easier to acquire than looks anyway. Being attractive comes from within. *Know that you're being judged at all times.* If you dress well, pay attention to your grooming, cultivate that smile, look good and cool at all times, and come across as friendly, warm, articulate, and caring, you will also come across as attractive and good looking. Looks are all in the smile and the eyes. Smiles that light up a room are magnetic and powerful. Eyes that twinkle and are full of life are enough to make us think the whole face is good looking.

Attractiveness is also about posture and position. If you slump you give off an aura of gloom and depression. This is unattractive and not good looking.

Your walk should be erect, proud, assured. So should your handshake. Everything about you should be up and open, happy and confident. This is attractive. Your grooming should be faultless, your dress sense superb, your style quirky but suave, your whole demeanor splendid and outstanding. This is attractive.

You do not

- Slouch
- Slump
- Look scruffy

You do

- Get anything fixed that can be fixed that would be considered unattractive—warts, bad breath, bad teeth, poor eyesight. (Stop squinting for God's sake and get some proper glasses!)

> ## LOOKS ARE ALL IN THE SMILE AND THE EYES.

Be Cool

At work you should retain your cool at all times and, no matter what, never ever lose your dignity. If there's an office costume party, you can laugh and joke with everyone else, but let them do the dressing up. You remain apart from all that office nonsense. Will this get you a reputation as standoffish? Arrogant? Self-important? Not if you're a Rules Player, because you'll know the Rules to make sure people admire, like, and respect you, without the need to dress up as Elvis or a fairy or whatever the theme is this year. Stay cool at all times. Give generously, support the cause, but leave the red noses for others to wear—at least when you're at work. Remain civilized and sophisticated at all times.

Let's face it, you are there to do a job. That's what they pay you for. You ain't there to make a fool of yourself. Just so long as you do that job—and do it well—the way you do it is up to you. You can choose to get involved in the social side of the office, or you can remain one step removed. This makes you one step away from your colleagues and thus one step nearer to being their manager.

None of this means you can't have a laugh and joke with your coworkers; just don't get so friendly or personal that it would become impossible to promote you above them. If you are going to be their boss soon, then it pays to keep a little bit of distance. And you do this by being cool.

If you don't know what cool is, try typing *cool* into your word processor and then, using the Thesaurus option, look for antonyms. You get: *warm, excited, unfashionable.* For warm, think sweaty hands—uncool. For excited, think small boy on Christmas Day—cute but uncool. For unfashionable think chunky cardigans—warm and uncool.

So we want to be

- Not warm—think not sweaty.
- Not excited—think not panicked.
- Not unfashionable—this isn't the same as fashionable but rather a timeless stylishness, which is, of course, completely different.

Cool operators are relaxed and in control. In a crisis they don't rush about screaming, but rather implement safety procedures and calmly and smoothly handle the situation. They are cool. They keep their heads and their composure. And invariably these are the people who others will turn to in a difficult situation. You don't want someone who panics; you want someone cool, calm, and collected.

> # REMAIN CIVILIZED
> # AND SOPHISTICATED
> # AT ALL TIMES.

RULE 22

Speak Well

So what does speaking well mean? Am I suggesting you walk around with a snooty voice and say "hice" instead of "house" and "creche" instead of "crash"? Of course not. You can keep your regional accent; that's not the problem. Look at why we speak—it is to communicate, to convey information—rather than how we speak. Speaking well means getting information across clearly and effectively. It doesn't matter how you speak, but it does matter that you speak clearly. And speaking clearly means just that—clearly. The things you must avoid are

- Mumbling—For obvious reasons, people can't hear or understand you.

- Speaking too softly or quietly—Again, people can't hear you.

- Using jargon—It's unintelligible to others outside your department or field of expertise.

- Any sort of speaking that identifies you with a particular group or social class—i.e. youth (trying to use the latest trendy slang or catchphrase), or politically extreme (radical anything, politically correct gone mad, ecologist, vegetarian, or environmentally obsessive), or too obviously belonging to any class system (too poor, too rich, too regional).

- Speaking badly—using "less" when you really mean "fewer"—that sort of thing. If you don't know the difference, get a grammar book and learn it by heart. Don't use verbal mannerisms such as "you know" or "like." Always finish your sentences.

RULE 22

There are four key words to remember to get you speaking well:

- Bright
- Clear
- Pleasant
- Simple

That's all you need to know. If you use these four, you won't go wrong, and people will remember what you say and be impressed by your clear, bright speaking voice. Speaking well makes an impact. If you slouch in and mumble your name, people will assume you are underconfident, ill at ease, and barely human—and thus quickly forget you. If you walk in confidently, say your name clearly and with confidence, people will assume you know where you are going, who you are, and what you want—and thus remember you. Speak simply—say directly what it is you want to say and nothing more.

> SPEAKING WELL MEANS
> GETTING INFORMATION
> ACROSS CLEARLY AND
> EFFECTIVELY.

RULE 23

Write Well

We write for two purposes. We write for others to read, and we write for ourselves to read. How you write for yourself is immaterial. You can scribble illegible shorthand or write like a five-year-old. It doesn't matter, just so long as no one else sees it. But how you write for others to read is of utmost and crucial importance. You will be judged on:

- What you write
- How your writing looks

Ah, but you say you don't write anything; you type everything. Fine. So what typeface do you choose, and why? What point size, and why? And you must have to sign documents—that's writing. Your signature is as open to judgment as anything else. I was once told that my signature was that of a very wealthy person. Good, although completely wrong, but it did indicate that I was getting close to the image I wanted to portray. A final point on this: always make your signature big—big signature, big person.

If you use handwriting a lot, then it needs to be

- Legible—It must be able to be read by everyone—or there simply is no point doing it and it is discourteous not to make the effort.
- Neat—No crossings out, all lines equal, that sort of thing.
- Stylish—A bit of a flourish here and there.
- Mature—Rounded letters and joined up.
- Consistent—The writing at the bottom of the page should look like the writing at the top of the page.

RULE 23

Watch your margins and the slope of your writing. You may not know it but margins—or signatures or any form of writing—that slope down towards the right of the page indicate a depressed person. Optimists slant upwards.

Make sure your spelling is correct and your grammar adequate—if not, study on it.

If you type a lot, use Times New Roman or Arial, 12 point, and only use italics or bold or underlining sparingly. Never mix typefaces—it betrays you as an unstable, immature personality, apparently—or point size. And you just thought it looked fun.

> HOW YOU WRITE FOR OTHERS TO READ IS OF UTMOST AND CRUCIAL IMPORTANCE.

PART III

HAVE
A PLAN

Do you know where you're going? If you don't, then the probability is that you'll end up going nowhere. Smart followers of *The Rules* know exactly where they're going. They have a plan. They have plotted the path to where they want to be—in six months, in a year, in five years. They've planned their game and know how to play. And so will you. Rules Players remain flexible and convert their plan according to circumstances—they're not rigid thinkers but smart and very fluid.

RULE 24

Know What You Want Long Term

So what's your game plan for your life? Don't know? Haven't ever thought about it? Most people don't. And that's why they fail. If you don't have a plan, it is terribly easy not to stick to it and end up where the current takes you—a bit of flotsam adrift on the eddies of life. Very sad. The Rules Player has a plan—long term and short term.

Long-term plans can be very simple—qualify, move up, reach the top, retire, die. Or they can be sensible and useful. If you intend to have a career, it makes sense to study the game plan of your chosen industry. Obviously, you will have to build in a certain contingency for the unexpected and the "out-of-your-control," but the shrewd Rules Player will have already amended their long-term game plan well in advance having seen the indicators and read the signs. I spoke to someone recently who said, "Who would have predicted downsizing then?" The answer is anyone with the brains to have seen which way their business sector was going.

So, study your chosen industry and see the progression steps needed to make it to the position you want to occupy. Work out what you need to make those steps. Work out how many steps it takes—usually no more than about four—junior, middle, senior, executive. (If you think otherwise, don't write in.)

Work out what you want from each step—gaining experience, handling responsibility, learning new skills, acquiring people management understanding, that sort of thing. You will notice that "increasing my earnings" just isn't an option here—that is a foregone conclusion if you are a Rules Player anyway.

RULE 24

Work out how each step is made. This might be a transfer to another department, relocation to another branch, being offered a partnership, being invited to join the board, moving to another company, that sort of thing. Once you know how each step is made, it doesn't take much to work out what you need to acquire that how.

You have to have an end game—the final goal. This can be as high or as extreme as you like—emperor of the world, prime minister, CEO, wealthiest person in the world, whatever. It is a dream and thus has no limits. If you set limits on your imagination, then you will have to settle for less than the best, less than perfect, less than you deserve. Ah, but you say we have to be realistic. Fine. Do that—be realistic. But Rules Players head for the very utmost of their dreams, and nothing less than the top is good enough.

> IF YOU DON'T HAVE A PLAN, IT IS TERRIBLY EASY NOT TO STICK TO IT AND END UP WHERE THE CURRENT TAKES YOU.

Know What You Want Short Term

How short is short term? That's entirely up to you. I have three short-term plans on the go—this month, this year, five years. This seems to provide me with sufficient information to plan my workload. It also allows me to work in, in the short term, plans that affect my family. I can allow for vacations, changes of school, garden/house projects and birthdays, Christmas, that sort of thing.

Your one-month short-term plan should obviously list current work projects—deadlines, prioritized tasks, basic routines. This is for work actually being carried out.

Your one-year plan should have projects that are being formulated, planned, presented, whatever. This is for work being planned rather than executed.

Your five-year plan should be for ideas, dreams, goals, wishes, wants; it is for work you intend executing one day.

Your long-term plan will have a career path built into it. Your five-year plan will take into it any steps you need to carry out that long-term plan.

I tend to keep three separate records for these three short-term plans. My one-month plan is kept on a clipboard on the desk. It contains a single sheet that lists boxes for deadlines, return phone calls, things to do. I suppose it's a bit like a calendar but without daily entries.

My one-year plan lives on the wall. It isn't a wall chart or year planner but, again, a single sheet with 12 boxes. In each box is a month with the relevant info of what I want to do during that time. It is what I *want* to do rather than what I *have* to do.

It is a short-term plan, not a to-do list or a calendar or a work schedule. As I am freelance, I have to generate work. This work—being done during my one-month plan or being generated during my one-year plan—is my bread and butter. It is made up of projects I want to do and projects I have to do. The ones I *have* to do are the bread and the ones I want to do are the butter—such as this book, which has been a delight to plan and write. My five-year plan is for my general direction—what sort of work do I want to be doing over the next five years? Your short-term plan will include work you have to do, but it will be mainly for work you want to do. The shorter the term, the more likely it is to read like your work schedule and less like a wish list.

All plans should include practical steps to put into action and make them happen. Otherwise they aren't "plans" but vague ideas.

Within any of these plans, you have to build a contingency. Someone phones you with a project; you can't turn it down on the basis that it isn't in your plan. You have to be flexible.

> ALL PLANS SHOULD INCLUDE PRACTICAL STEPS TO PUT INTO ACTION AND MAKE THEM HAPPEN.

RULE 26

Study the Promotion System

When you start your career, it is at the lowest level, and you gaze upward at the boss, the manager, the managing director, with reverence and awe. One day, inevitably, you will age, gain experience, and ascend to greater heights yourself. Either that or maybe start up on your own. And for most people that's about it. Career-wise they meander vaguely upward, often getting sidetracked and stopping at a level where they seem comfortable, coasting, happy. And that's it. Career over. Game over. Very sad. Unless that's really what you want. And if you're a committed Rules Player, I doubt it.

The Rules Player never meanders or arrives anywhere vaguely. You plan. You know the system and use it. You understand the steps to be taken to get you from A to B and onward and upward all the way to Z.

You have to study the promotion system if you are to enter it and profit from it. It is simply no use waiting for something to turn up, or for fate to take a hand and propel you upward by luck or chance. You have to seize the day and make your own luck. You have to know exactly how to avoid all clichés and elevate yourself within the system.

So, what is the promotion system within your industry? Do you know it? Have you studied it? Study the background of others who have been there before you. If not, chances are you are relying on luck to get you somewhere. This may be fine, and it may get you where you want to be, but it is unreliable— bit like playing the lottery in the hope it'll make you rich and you can retire. It might happen, but it's not likely.

Making a promotion chart:

- Within your industry look upward to the most senior position that can be held (or the highest you could possibly expect yourself to aim for—they should really be the same thing—mark this).
- Now look at the lowest—mark this.
- Now plot all the steps in-between.
- Now mark your own place.
- Now list the steps needed to get there.

You now have your own promotion chart and can cross off each step as you make it.

(The same principle of steps also works if you decide that rather than ascend where you are, you'd like to go up on your own and be entrepreneurial rather than corporate.)

While you are doing this, you can also list all the skills/experience, etc. that you would need for each step to be made successfully. Next to this, you can add what you have to do to acquire these—where you must go, what you have to learn, what you need to study. You can add these back into your long-term plan and your five-year plan.

> ## YOU HAVE TO SEIZE THE DAY AND MAKE YOUR OWN LUCK.

RULE 27

Develop a Game Plan

Developing a game plan is a bit like an actor choosing a part and learning their script. Your game plan has to be who you are going to be. Not many people choose consciously to be a loser, but that's where they end up. Don't let it happen to you. And it doesn't happen, once you seize the initiative and develop a game plan.

Your game plan is a sort of personal mission statement. It is different from setting objectives, which is how to be the person your game plan decides you are.

So who are you going to be? Successful? A failure? Someone who gives up? Someone who picks themselves up, dusts themselves off, and starts all over again? A brilliant career strategist? A loser? None of these?

Obviously, you could decide to be ruthless, unpleasant, cruel, vindictive, but we assume you won't—a Rules Player is never any of these. Your game plan should include your qualities as well as what sort of game you want to plan—"I will be successful and still be a thoroughly nice person."

Not many people sit down and consciously carry out this exercise. It may seem simple, but it is an essential tool to get you to where you want to be. If more people did this, they wouldn't end up as idiots, or the office bore, or a gossip, or frighteningly callous in their dealings with their colleagues. If we all had to sit down and write our game plan—and then live by it—we might all end up as nicer people. There is no bad karma in trying your hardest to be pleasant, cooperative, helpful, friendly, kind, and honest in your dealings with others around you. Who would sit down and write, "I am going to be a complete and utter bastard and harm as many people as I can, be disliked by everyone, and generally make myself as unpopular as possible"? Yes, no one would write it, but I've worked with quite a few who live by it as a game plan. Yes, they may be successful, but how do they sleep at night? How do they live with themselves?

I once worked with a fairly senior manager whose technique was to arrive, walk through the department, bawl out as many people as he could, go to his office, put his feet up with a coffee for half an hour and then walk back again being as nice as pie to everyone. When I questioned him about this, he said, "It keeps them on their toes. They never know where they are with me." He was genuinely disliked by everyone, feared by most, and commanded zero respect from his peers. Good game plan. Not.

> NOT MANY PEOPLE CHOOSE CONSCIOUSLY TO BE A LOSER, BUT THAT'S WHERE THEY END UP.

Set Objectives

An objective is a simple one-sentence mission statement that you can use to get you through your day. It is almost impossible to be successful or to get promoted if you don't set objectives.

An objective outlines the key important ingredients in your work recipe. Suppose you have a meeting to go to. Now we all hate meetings—they are interminable, boring, unproductive, counter-productive—and an endless source of irritation and argument. You know that Stephen from accounts is going to be there and will endeavor—usually successfully—to wind you up. You know you'll get sidetracked and end up discussing the relocation to Swindon when it doesn't even affect your department. You know you'll end up discussing budgets for the exhibition stand when that's six months away and it hasn't even been decided that you're going to take a stand at the NEC this year. So, set an objective:

> "I will speak only on matters I know about and understand and are relevant to me at this meeting, and no matter what Stephen does, I shall not rise to the bait."

Good. Now stick to it.

Suppose you have to present a report to the Finance Committee about the new costs of the wildflower meadow to go in front of head office's new buildings. You know the Finance Committee can waffle on for hours about irrelevant topics such as whether it is better to have oxeye daises or marsh buttercups, and all you need to do is present them with the cost of seeds, mowing equipment, and haymaking provisions without getting caught up in the minutiae of which flower is most attractive in spring. So, set an objective:

> "I will present my report and, once comments have been made, will make my excuses and leave. If the committee insist on discussing matters that are irrelevant to my being there I shall assertively point this out and leave."

Good. Now stick to it.

Use an objective for every area of your working life. Objectives take but seconds, but they do help highlight

- What is wrong
- Solutions to what is wrong
- Action to be taken to correct what is wrong
- Ways to prevent the problem recurring

> ## IT IS ALMOST IMPOSSIBLE TO BE SUCCESSFUL OR TO GET PROMOTED IF YOU DON'T SET OBJECTIVES.

Know Your Role

What is your role? I know you are there to do a job, carry out a function, perform certain tasks, follow set procedures, and all that. But what is your role? This is a bit like setting a game plan. A game plan outlines what sort of working person you are going to be. A role is what sort of facilitator you will be. Will you be an ideas person? A moderator? A communicator? A diplomat? A task master? A motivator? Basically, your role is how you fit into the team—and yes, we are all team players; we have to be in this day and age.

Dr. Meredith Belbin has spent over 20 years researching the nature of team work to improve people's strengths. He has identified nine distinct team roles:

- Plant—They are original thinkers; they generate new ideas; they offer solutions to problems; they think in radically different ways, laterally, imaginatively.

- Resource Investigator—They are creative; they like to take ideas and run with them; they are extroverted and popular.

- Coordinator—They are highly disciplined and controlled; they can focus on objectives; they unify a team.

- Shaper—They are very achievement orientated; they like to be challenged and to get results.

- Monitor Evaluator—They analyze and balance and weigh; they are calm and detached; they are objective thinkers.

- Team Worker—They are supportive and cooperative; they make good diplomats as they only want what is best for the team.

- Implementer—They have good organizational skills; they display common sense; they like to get the job done.
- Completer—They check details; they tidy up after them; they are painstakingly conscientious.
- Specialist—They are dedicated to acquiring a specialized skill; they are extremely professional; they have drive and dedication.

So which are you? What role do you play in the team? Are you happy with your role? Can you change it?

BASICALLY, YOUR ROLE IS HOW YOU FIT INTO THE TEAM—AND YES, WE ARE ALL TEAM PLAYERS; WE HAVE TO BE IN THIS DAY AND AGE

Know Yourself—Strengths and Weaknesses

If you are going to be a Rules Player, you have to be incredibly objective about yourself. A lot of people can't do this; they can't turn the spotlight on themselves objectively enough or brightly enough to see themselves as others see them. And it's not just how others see us; it's also how we see ourselves. We all carry a mental image of ourselves—what we look like and sound like, what makes us tick; how we work—but how realistic is this image? I think I work creatively and eccentrically; others think I am messy and unorganized. Which is true? Which is the reality?

To know your strengths and weaknesses, you first have to understand your role—the way you work. I might see being creative as a strength—lots of lovely ideas, no attention to detail, generating new projects rather than seeing them through or actually working on them—surely all these are strengths? Not if I am a Completer or Implementer they're not; then they are weaknesses. Instead, my strengths would be perseverance, diligence, stickability, predictability, conformity, steadfastness, orderliness—yuk, surely these are weaknesses? You have to know your role before you can make subjective judgments about strengths and weaknesses.

If in doubt, make lists; that's what I always say. Write down what you think are your strengths and weaknesses. Show this list to a close friend who you do not work with. Ask for their objective evaluation. Now show it to someone you can trust who you do work with. Is there a difference in their evaluation of how close to the truth you are? Bet there is quite a difference. This is because the special skills you bring to friendships are quite different from the ones you bring to a work relationship.

This rule is about knowing your strengths and weaknesses; it isn't necessarily about improving them, eliminating them, working on them, changing them in any way. What we are is what we are, and it is what we have to work with. You may well be disorganized, erratic, unpredictable—is this good or bad? It all depends on your role. You may need to change your role to suit your strengths and weaknesses better.

A lot of people think that identifying their strengths and weaknesses means they get to lose the bad stuff and only work with the good stuff. Not true. This isn't therapy. This is the real world. We all have weaknesses. The secret trick is learning to work with them rather than trying to be perfect, which is unrealistic and unproductive.

You might be able to find better uses for your weaknesses—but then they would become strengths, wouldn't they? Think about it.

> YOU HAVE TO KNOW YOUR ROLE BEFORE YOU CAN MAKE SUBJECTIVE JUDGMENTS ABOUT STRENGTHS AND WEAKNESSES.

Identify Key Times and Events

A cobra has a lot of power, a lot of venom, a lot of energy. But how often do you see one strike? Rarely. Cobras only use all that power and energy when it is

- Appropriate
- Meaningful
- Advantageous
- Beneficial
- Necessary
- Important

They strike when in danger or when they need to feed. The rest of the time you wouldn't know they were there. The rest of the time they don't even look like cobras. They don't display their hood except when they have to. You will become a cobra. There is no point using all your energy and power when it ain't necessary. What you have to do is identify the key times and events—then you strike.

A cobra's key times and events are fairly simple to identify— threat and hunger. But what are yours? Much more difficult.

There's not a lot of point burning all that midnight oil to produce a report that only a couple of your colleagues get to see and is then forgotten. Wait until it's the big report that's going straight to the desk of the president—that's the one that needs the cobra's striking force.

Of course, a lot of people wait for the key time—the office party, the key exhibition—and then they completely and utterly screw it up. They get drunk or fluff their lines, they are late or sick, or they appear with their flies undone or their skirts tucked into the back of their underwear.

And key events? The presentation is a good one. Get it right and it's remembered. Get it wrong and it's you that is forgotten.

You don't get it wrong. Identify these times and events and shine at them. Be a cobra and strike when it is appropriate.

> THERE IS NO POINT USING ALL YOUR ENERGY AND POWER WHEN IT AIN'T NECESSARY.

RULE 32

Anticipate Threats

Threats come at us from every quarter, every day—redundancy, downsizing, takeovers, vindictive colleagues, irascible bosses, new technology, new systems, new procedures. In fact, entire books are devoted to threats—mostly from change—such as Who Moved My Cheese? and How to Handle Tough Situations at Work. If we can think on our feet, stay out of ruts, be flexible and move fast, roll with the punches, and go the distance, we will not only survive change but we shall also be contortionists and athletes of the highest order. Of course, we can't do all that. There will be times when the threat will overtake us and we get squashed. It happens to us all. There is no getting away from the fact that life gets fired at us at point blank range, and we rarely if ever get time to duck.

But a threat is always that. Once it becomes a reality, we can deal with it. While it is still a threat, it induces fear but can do no harm. Spotting which threat will turn into a reality is the skill. The talent. There are many threats, and we can't react to all of them. There are fewer realities, and we have to react to them.

It helps if we don't see threats as threats, but instead as opportunities. Each threat that becomes a reality is an opportunity to grow and change, adapt and rework our methods and style of management. If our attitude is positive, we tend to see threats less as a negative thing and more as a positive thing—they bring us the chance to prove ourselves. If we never get challenged, we will never improve.

I was once employed as a manager by a company that was taken over. The new bosses brought in their own managers, and three of us were "downgraded"—demoted in other words. We had no choice—apart from walking out, of course. I was, by this time, a committed Rules Player, so I saw it as an opportunity to prove to the new bosses that I was good enough to be one of their managers and, three months later, I was back up there.

Of the other two, one eventually walked and one stayed "downgraded." They both bitched and moaned and felt the move was derogatory and demeaning and an insult. It probably was, but I didn't need to feel depressed about it. I needed to get back up there—upward and onward.

> EACH THREAT THAT BECOMES A REALITY IS AN OPPORTUNITY TO GROW AND CHANGE.

Look for Opportunities

I know I've said have a plan—both long term and short term—but there do come times when plans have to be thrown out of the window. These are the opportunities. I had a friend who wasn't getting on particularly fast in his promotion plan. One day he found himself sharing a compartment on the train with his chairman. This was his opportunity. He could have fluffed his lines, made a jackass of himself, or been too embarrassed or nervous to take the advantage. But he didn't do any of these things. He made his pitch perfectly. All he did was to chat informally but with the respect his chairman warranted; show a keen grasp of the company's history, mission statement, and general aims; be presentable, smart, and well spoken; express himself clearly and articulately; and, most importantly, didn't noticeably press his advantage—he knew when to shut up and back off. It certainly worked. His department head was told by the chairman that she had a "Smart young man there—bring him on a bit, will you?" What choice did she have but to promote him?

That's seizing an opportunity. You can't write that into your plan, and these moments will come along. When they do you must

- Recognize them
- Play them well
- Be cool and suave

What you mustn't do is

- Fail to recognize the moment for what it is—a fleeting opportunity

- Panic
- Over play your hand
- Get so excited you make a idiot of yourself

Learn to see opportunities as balls—if they get thrown your way, you have but a split second to catch them. There is no time for asking questions, looking over your shoulder, weighing the pros and cons, or dancing the foxtrot. You either catch the ball or you don't.

Spend a little time looking back at what opportunities you have missed—and what you would do if you had the same chance a second time. Would you react differently now? What did you do wrong?

> LEARN TO SEE
> OPPORTUNITIES AS
> BALLS—IF THEY GET
> THROWN YOUR WAY,
> YOU HAVE BUT A SPLIT
> SECOND TO
> CATCH THEM.

Make Learning a Lifelong Mission

I met a guy once who came from a very poor background and was unable to take his education as far as he'd have liked. He left school at 14 and ended up working all his life as a customs officer, working his way up to a middle management role. When he retired at 65, he decided that at last he could afford to get the education he'd always wanted. So he got a law degree, did his training, and qualified as a barrister at the age of about 70. How many of us would have the attitude to learning you need to do that? (Never mind the energy!)

When you watch kids learn, you can see how much they enjoy it. Not when it's boring rote learning with tedious teachers, of course, but when they're inspired and motivated they couldn't be happier. Well, you and I still have the same brain we had when we were kids. OK, we may have lost a few little grey cells, but we can still enjoy learning. And if we don't keep learning, we stagnate and become boring old stick-in-the-muds. If you don't learn, you can't change, and if you aren't changing, what's the point of being here?

So, make it your express purpose to keep learning. I know a teacher in Scotland who dreamed as a child of becoming a spaceman—like most of his school friends no doubt. However, he did something about it and, instead of allowing everyday life to get in the way of his aim, he lifted his head and made a point of learning and developing.

As a result, he won a scholarship to the U.S. Space and Rocket Center in Alabama for a week's intensive space training, complete with zero-gravity exercises and simulated shuttle take-offs. How cool is that? After that he could pursue his dream of taking this knowledge and passing it onto the pupils he now teaches. All because he approached life as an ongoing lesson.

We can all learn* from people like him. Remember what it was that inspired you as a child? Or consider the new things that have grabbed your interest since. Learning new skills for work is valuable, from another language to new computer software. But any learning keeps your mind open and free and exercised, which will benefit your work and your employer. So, whatever it is that excites you, go on—make it your aim to learn more about it.

> IF YOU DON'T LEARN, YOU CAN'T CHANGE, AND IF YOU AREN'T CHANGING, WHAT'S THE POINT OF BEING HERE?

* And if we do, we'll be following this Rule already

PART IV

IF YOU CAN'T SAY ANYTHING NICE— SHUT UP

These are really easy Rules to understand but tough to follow. We all like to gossip, to bitch, to talk about our boss behind her back. The Rule, however, is—don't do it. Learn to say only positive things, nice things, complimentary things. People judge you by what you say as much as how you say it, so be known as someone who is always pleasant and upbeat.

Don't Gossip

"Did you know that at the last company conference Steve, from accounts, was seen coming out of Debbie's, from marketing, bedroom in the early hours of Sunday morning? And that twice since they have been seen in Luigi's at lunchtime, and Kathy swears she's seen them holding hands in the lift. Steve's married, you know, and I thought Debbie was engaged. What do you think? Should they be carrying on like this?"

Answer: "What's this got to do with me?"

Good, it has nothing to do with you, unless Steve happens to be your boss and his work is being affected, or you happen to be Debbie's fiancé. This Rule says that you don't gossip. It doesn't say you don't listen. You may find it interesting, and knowing what's going on comes in useful sometimes. But there is one part of this Rule that is really, really simple—don't pass anything on. That's it. Gossip stops with you. If you listen but don't pass it along or offer an opinion, you'll be seen as "one of us" rather than a party pooper. You don't have to be seen disapproving—merely don't pass anything along.

Gossiping is the occupation of idle minds—those who haven't got enough work to do. It is also the domain of workers who have mindless jobs to do—jobs they can do without thinking and thus have to occupy themselves with inane chatter, rumors, lies, and malicious stories. Trouble is that if you don't join in, you can be seen as severe or stuck-up. You have to look as if you gossip without ever doing it. Don't go getting all self-righteous and telling everyone how silly they are doing it.

With most things, discretion is the key word. Don't be seen disapproving—just don't do it, and keep that to yourself.

> THERE IS ONE PART OF THIS RULE THAT IS REALLY, REALLY SIMPLE—DON'T PASS ANYTHING ON.

Don't Bitch

Yep, life ain't fair. Sometimes colleagues shirk and you end up with extra work; bosses can be ill prepared for their jobs and as such are incompetent and often inconsistent; idiots get promoted all around you; there's too much work to do; there are too many stupid systems in place; idiots thwart you at every turn. It's true—life's a bitch.

Now tell me how moaning helps in any one of these scenarios. Tell me how moaning will change one single thing. It won't. It doesn't. Moaning is a time-wasting device invented by sad people who haven't enough work to do. And they're usually the ones standing next to the ones gossiping. They may even be the same ones—chances are they are. And when they've finished having a good moan, they'll have a good gossip.

Moaning is pointless. It is unproductive and achieves nothing. All it does is

- Identifies you as idle, petty, trivial
- Encourages you to turn the corners of your mouth down—not attractive
- Wastes time
- Makes you a magnet for other moaners
- Gets you a reputation as someone who doesn't offer anything productive or helpful
- Demotivates you and sets up a vicious circle

So, what are you going to do if you are a habitual moaner? Easy, make sure that whenever you do moan you make yourself offer a solution to whatever it is you are moaning about. If you can't see a solution, you aren't allowed to moan. Try that for a few weeks, and you'll stop moaning quite naturally.

Bitching about others invariably takes place behind their backs. Next time you feel the need for a good bitch about someone, make yourself go and do it to their face. If they aren't present in the room, don't do it. Simple Rule, but it works. Once they are there, you'll stop bitching; it's too hard to keep doing it when you've upset everyone in the office. If you've got something to say, say it to their face (but do see the introduction to this Rule first—*If you can't say anything nice— shut up*).

> MOANING IS POINTLESS.
> IT IS UNPRODUCTIVE AND
> ACHIEVES NOTHING.

RULE 37

Compliment People Sincerely

The key to this Rule is "sincerely." You mustn't use compliments glibly, falsely, shallowly, dishonestly, or disingenuously. Compliments must be real, honest, open, guileless and meaningful.

Being the sort of person who gives compliments is quite tricky. You don't want to be seen as a slimeball or spooky—and people who do give compliments can often end up seen like this—but you do want to come across as genuinely warm and friendly.

So how to do this? And why? Well, if you do it affably, it makes people think incredibly well about you—it is good office karma. The best way to do it is by being unsophisticated about it. All you have to do is say, "I really like the way you've had your hair cut," and then ask a question about whatever it is you are complimenting her on, and make it about how it was done. "So who did your hair?"

> "I do like the way you handled that customer; how did you feel saying that?"

> "I must say I liked your report; how is it going down with the board?"

Try to avoid using over-the-top expressions. You don't love their new coat—you merely "like" it. Remember, if you "love" it, you'll want to marry it and have its babies. Not true of a coat, or a report, or a hair style, or the way someone handles a customer.

If you "like" something, feel free to say so. You can emphasize how much you like something by

- "I really like ..."
- "I do like ..."
- "Can I tell you how much I liked ...?"
- And it doesn't just have to be "liked," although it is a very good one to start with
- "I was impressed by ..."
- "I thought you did really well ..."
- "The way you did ... was very good indeed"
- "I did enjoy your presentation. It was really rather exceptional."

When giving compliments, make sure you can't be accused of flirting or coming on to someone—keep it professional and/or work related. I'm sure you don't need telling this.

> BEING THE SORT OF PERSON WHO GIVES COMPLIMENTS IS QUITE TRICKY.

RULE 38

Stand Up for Others

So, you're all sitting round having coffee when the subject of young Adam comes up. Now we all know that Adam is a pain in the backside. He doesn't pull his weight, goofs off, steals the pens and paperclips, is rude to the security staff, always off-loads as much work onto others as possible, blames others for his mistakes, and is generally obnoxious. So you all have a moan about him behind his back, and get a lot of your anger about his behaviour off your chest. But you don't. Oh, the others might but you won't, not from now on. You are now a Rules Player, and you stand up for others.

No matter how obnoxious young Adam is, you will always find something nice—and genuine—to say about him. That is your objective—find something nice to say no matter what.

At first this may be quite hard, but if you persevere it becomes increasingly easy—it's all a question of habit and mental outlook. If we are used to bitching and moaning, then that's what we do. But if we change our approach, we can be more positive—though it does take a bit of effort initially to make this change.

Standing up for others, no matter what, gets you a reputation as someone who can always find something nice to say about everybody. Thus, those who you would have moaned about know that you, of all the work force, will always be fighting their corner for them. It gets you unwritten loyalty and a sort of guardian angel relationship with the more unpopular members of the team.

This is a strange relationship to have, but it works wonders— these are the people who will back you in an emergency. They will let you know if someone is trying to mess you up. They will pull out all the stops for you because they know you care. If you need a favor, they will be the ones to call on.

It's amazing how quickly the word will spread that you are a thoroughly nice person—you don't bitch, you don't moan, you stand up for the underdog, you are supportive, and you can always see at least one good point in a thoroughly bad apple.

Obviously, you will have to do this in an honest and sincere fashion—it's no good lying or making it up. If you, at first, simply can't find anything positive to say, then shut up. But there is always something nice to say—nobody is completely evil or wicked or nasty.

So, back to young Adam. What are you going to say? Well, for a start you could point out that he makes good coffee. Or that he is always on time. Or he is very good at handling irate customers. Or he has a brilliant sense of humor. Or he always knows the football scores. Just keep saying "But he's good because he ..."

> IT GETS YOU UNWRITTEN
> LOYALTY AND A SORT OF
> GUARDIAN ANGEL
> RELATIONSHIP WITH THE
> MORE UNPOPULAR
> MEMBERS OF THE TEAM.

RULE 39

Be Cheerful and Positive

If you go into work each morning with a positive vibe, it sets you up as the sort of person to whom stress and troubles and problems are but as water off a duck's back. You thus get a reputation as being someone who is in control, smooth, relaxed, confident, and very mature. And all for the sake of a few bars of "Moon River," whistled as you make your way to your desk.

Be cheerful at all times. So it's raining out there and it's a dark and depressing winter's afternoon. Business is slack, interest rates have just gone up again and the boss is in a foul mood, and everyone's keeping their heads down. It's still no reason to lose your smile. So it's a bad day; this too will pass, and the sun will come back. Whatever your situation, things will always get better.

Maintaining a cheerful and positive outlook is a trick. At first you don't have to believe it—just do it. Act it. Pretend. But do it. After a little while you'll find it isn't an act, you're not pretending, you genuinely do feel cheerful. It's a trick. You are tricking yourself, no one else. Putting on a smile triggers hormones. These hormones will make you feel better. Once you feel better, you will smile more and thus produce more hormones. All it takes is the first few days smiling when you don't feel like it, and you will start a cycle going that will make you feel better all the time.

Once you are seen as someone cheerful and positive, people will want to hang out with you more—there is nothing so attractive as a cheerful person.

Bring some flowers into work and brighten up your desk. Whistle. Smile. Laugh. Never reveal that you feel like the pits inside. It's all too easy when someone says, "How are you?" to reply "Oh, OK, I guess, can't complain, mustn't grumble, you know, struggling on." It's a cliché. It's a habit. Try instead, "Fine, really good actually, doing OK." There's a trick for you.

So someone brings you more work that you simply have to do—it's unavoidable and part of your remit, and just when you thought you could see a little light at the end of the tunnel. Easy to say, "Oh no, not more bloody work. Can't everybody see how busy I am? This really is too much." If it's unavoidable and moaning isn't going to change a thing, then maybe saying, "Fine, just dump it there; I'll get on with it in a moment. Thanks." Why berate the messenger? I'm sure he didn't personally generate all this extra work just to piss you off. So it's a drag having extra work to do. So what? So be cheerful and get on with it. Every second spent moaning and bitching is a second taken off your life. Every second spent being cheerful and positive is a second added on. Take your choice.

> SO IT'S A BAD DAY;
> THIS TOO WILL PASS, AND
> THE SUN WILL COME BACK.

RULE 40

Ask Questions

The object of the exercise is to become:

- Popular
- Promotable
- Successful
- Thoroughly nice
- Efficient

One of the easiest ways to do this is to learn and practice the habit of asking questions. What sort of questions? Well, that depends, obviously on the situation. For instance, in Rule 38: Compliment people sincerely, we used a couple of examples where the follow-up question is useful—"I really liked your presentation. I thought you were incredibly calm. How do you avoid shaking?" Or—"I like your new method of handling invoices. What gave you the idea?"

Asking questions shows that you have paid attention, care, are interested, are thoughtful, are considerate and intelligent and creative. Stupid people don't ask questions. Bored people don't ask questions. Lazy people don't ask questions. Any questions?

Belligerent people tend to make statements—"I don't like that idea; it's unworkable." Rules Players ask questions; they might mean the same thing, but they handle it differently—"I think I need more information about this idea. How do you see it working? Will dispatch be able to handle the increase in orders? Can we provide enough extra staff to cover? Maybe we all need to go away and think about this one. What does everyone else think?" You haven't said the idea stinks, but they know you think that but they also think you're a thoroughly nice person—you haven't shot them down in flames in front of their colleagues, but you have given them enough rope to hang themselves if they want to. And you've given them a way out if they choose to take it—go away and think about it a bit more means let's not hear about this again, but it's a terribly diplomatic way of saying so.

Asking questions is a very nice thing to do in a general way. It shows you are interested in your colleagues. But do make the questions genuine and sincere, worthwhile and kind.

There's very little point in asking, "Where on earth did you get that coat? You can't think it suits you, surely?" Much better not to dwell on the coat if it really is horrid. Ask instead about the work: "How come you can always do this invoicing so quickly? Do you have some secret the rest of us don't have?"

As in the case of standing up for someone—even if they are loathsome, there will always be some good point about a person; no one is totally wicked—so too with questions. There will always be some aspect of someone's work that you could ask about or their hobbies or social life or family. Even if it's a simple "How are the kids?", it cuts the ice and makes you nice. It opens up dialogue, generates pleasantness, and creates warmth among people who have to work together every day.

> ## IT SHOWS YOU ARE INTERESTED IN YOUR COLLEAGUES.

Use "Please" and "Thank You"

You would have thought this one so obvious, so basic, and so fundamental that surely it can't be part of the Rules. Sorry, but we all need reminding that saying "please" and "thank you" is terribly important. It just doesn't happen enough. People say that they are too busy or too forgetful, or that it should be taken as read that they have said them and they don't need to each and every time. Rubbish. The only reason please and thank you get forgotten is plain old bad manners. If we start ignoring even the basic levels of human decency and politeness, then there really is no point to any of us being here. If we aren't civil and civilized enough to thank someone, or to be bothered enough to say "please," then it really is time to pack it in.

It doesn't matter how many times a day someone passes you a piece of paper—it is "thank you" every single time without fail or exception. It doesn't matter how many times you have to ask for the same thing—you always say "please." If someone does anything for you, no matter how mundane, trivial, repetitive, boring, effortless, you will always say thank you.

You forget one time, and you will be labeled as rude, boorish, and unpleasant. Make someone's day and don't forget, please. Thank you. I once worked with a manager who could get staff to work the graveyard shift, come in on their holidays, work overtime, work their days off, take work home with them, work on weekends, and work harder than any other manager could. We all watched him, trying to work out what it was he was doing that we weren't. He was getting loyalty from his team that we weren't. I know you are ahead of me at this stage and have got your hand up with the answer. He said "please" and "thank you."

Yes. Happy now? He did indeed. And that simple bit of politeness went a long way. I don't think his staff consciously knew he did it. We certainly couldn't spot it for a long time. Most of us reckoned we also said "please" and "thank you." But he said it without fail every single time. And when you say it, mean it. A sincere and warm thank you goes a long way. It is also a very good way to respond to compliments and praise yourself. If someone says you have done something well, don't blush and stammer, "It was nothing really." That subtracts from their compliment. Better instead just to say, "Thank you." Never use the word "please" to wheedle or cajole. It is "Could you work through this lunchtime, please, as we need extra cover on the phones? I'll make sure you get the time back a bit later this afternoon." It is not, "*Pleeeeease* can you work, pretty *pleeeease*."

> A SINCERE AND WARM
> THANK YOU GOES A
> LONG WAY.

Don't Swear

I know we all do it. I know you think it's cool. I know we have to be modern and move with the times. But I'm sorry, swearing isn't allowed. You can say what you want when you get home, or in the car on your own. But at work you don't swear. It's a simple Rule, but it works because it is a default setting—you don't swear. Now what decisions and choices do you have to make about that? Answer: None. None whatsoever. It is your bottom line. You don't swear, so all the tricky stuff has been taken away from you.

But if swearing is your default setting, you have so many decisions and choices to make, I'm surprised you get any work done at all. For instance do you:

- Swear every time something goes wrong
- Swear over the phone
- Swear in front of the boss
- Swear in front of customers
- Swear at customers
- Limit yourself to certain swear words and not use others
- Use religious blasphemy as swear words
- Limit yourself to mild swearing or go for the really offensive

RULE 42

It's a mine field. It's a nightmare. It really is so much easier to just not bother. This isn't a puritan dictate. It is an efficiency dictate. It saves time and effort and having to think about it if you simply don't do it. Now go away.

> YOU CAN SAY WHAT YOU
> WANT WHEN YOU GET
> HOME, OR IN THE CAR
> ON YOUR OWN.
> BUT AT WORK
> YOU DON'T SWEAR.

RULE 43

Be a Good Listener

I don't mean you should provide a nice padded shoulder for all and sundry to come and cry on. In fact, that probably isn't good listening but therapy. A good listener is someone who makes the speaker know that they are listening. You do this by:

- Making encouraging noises—"Hmmm, go on, yes, I'm listening."
- Displaying appropriate body language—Head tilted to one side, eyes open, and looking at the person speaking, not yawning or fiddling with your watch.
- Repeating back some bits to make sure they know you've taken them in— "On Friday at 3, yes, I've got that."
- Getting them to repeat things you haven't heard or understood—"Can you repeat that bit about Peterborough? I'm not sure I was taking that in."
- Asking questions—"So the move to Gloucester will not happen now?"
- Taking notes—Write stuff down as they speak.

Now why would you want to be a good listener? I said, now why would you want to be a good listener? Easy. You get

- More facts
- A better understanding of what you are supposed to be doing
- A better grasp of what is going on around you
- Seen as sympathetic and considerate
- Seen as intelligent and alert
- Seen as someone on top of their job

If you don't listen, you don't know. If you are going to listen, make sure they know you are. Easy.

Good listening is a skill, a special talent, that you will have to practice and learn. It doesn't happen overnight, and it isn't automatic. You have to think about it and catch yourself when you aren't listening and turn it on then.

> GOOD LISTENING IS A
> SKILL, A SPECIAL TALENT,
> THAT YOU WILL HAVE TO
> PRACTICE AND LEARN.

RULE 44

Only Speak Sense

To become successful and get promoted, you have to project the right image—the wise, mature, reliable, cool, sophisticated, trustworthy, experienced business person—and there are times when all the hard work can be devastated, destroyed, by a careless word or unguarded moment. Recently, a shadow government front-bench minister was sacked because she told a "racist" joke at a rugby club dinner. Her career was brought down by an unguarded moment of not "speaking sense."

You have to guard your tongue against:

- Un-PC comments
- Offensive jokes or remarks that alienate any section of the community
- Sexism in any form
- Patronizing people
- Arrogance
- Loss of temper
- Offensive swearing—*see Rule 42*
- Bitching, moaning, gossiping—*see Rules 35, 36, and 37*
- Revealing what you really think of people

It might be wise to learn to speak only occasionally, rather than chattering on. If you let your tongue run away with itself, it is so much more likely that you'll say the wrong thing. If you think carefully before you speak, pause, and have a chance to bite your tongue, then the chances are that your delivery will be accurate, your speech edited carefully, and you will only speak sense. You thus get a reputation for being wise and mature. People will come to you for advice and guidance because they know you think about what you are going to say and don't just chatter on. They will trust you. Once trusted, you are a natural candidate for promotion and success.

Make sure that what you have to say has an impact and isn't lost in the general hubbub of office clamor. Don't chat about what you watched on TV last night—to be honest no one is really interested—instead be silent until you have something of import to offer.

> THERE ARE TIMES WHEN ALL THE HARD WORK CAN BE DEVASTATED, DESTROYED, BY A CARELESS WORD OR UNGUARDED MOMENT.

PART V

LOOK AFTER
YOURSELF

Most people you deal with are probably decent and good to be around. However, there are always a few who aren't. You can't avoid them—the bastards, the jealous colleagues, the ones who will take any opportunity to stab you in the back or do you harm. They'll shoot you down in flames at any chance they get. Make sure that your new image doesn't make you a target. These Rules are about minimizing enemies and staying one jump ahead. As you get more successful, it is often a sort of organic process that you attract jealousy and envy. By practicing these Rules, you will avoid this and look after yourself—especially your back.

Know the Ethics of Your Industry

So, what do you do for a living? I don't mean the actual job. I mean what contribution do you make to society? Is your contribution positive, beneficial, healthy? Or is it detrimental, negative, damaging? What does your industry do? How much a part of that industry are you? Have you considered the ethics of your industry?

What do we mean by ethics? Ethics are the morals of your industry—the rights and wrongs, the good and bad. Is your industry a good thing or a bad thing? Does it hurt or heal? Is it putting something positive into society or merely taking something out?

No, you don't have to walk out if you have just suddenly decided that your own particular industry stinks. What you can do is work from the inside to change things. I don't think we're talking environmental issues here, although I am aware that they may be of concern to a lot of us. Instead, I want you to concentrate on what your industry does morally.

Obviously, if you do decide that your industry is unjustified in its approach—and this happened to me and I walked—and you simply cannot live with it, then you have to get out. This is good karma, and you gain benefit even if you do lose out financially.

Within your industry there will be good bits and bad bits. Occasionally, you will be asked to cross the line and do bad things. Obviously, you will have read *Rule 47: Set Personal Standards* but this is about helping set standards for your industry rather than personal ones. You have to point out that morally, ethically, what you are being asked to do is bad for the company. Constantly say, "What would the press do if they got hold of this?" and offer them a suitable headline: "Scrooge Ltd replaces sacked workers with Asian sweatshop labor."

Yes, you can be as assertive as you like and refuse, but you might just get labelled then as a wimp who is frightened to get his hands dirty—no guts, that sort of thing. No, you have to point out the ramifications for the company. You have to implant the idea of the whistle blower—"Hey, what would they do with this?" This way you will be one of the company people while still playing the ethics card. You will be one of us and one of them all at the same time.

To do all this, you have to know the ethics of your industry and know what its contribution is. Do your research now.

> IS YOUR INDUSTRY A GOOD THING OR A BAD THING? DOES IT HURT OR HEAL?

RULE 46

Know the Legalities of Your Industry

Is your company breaking any laws? Are you breaking any laws? Do you know the legalities of your industry?

I once worked for an organization that was, initially, remarkably above board. It prided itself on being a standard setter, a new thing in the industry. After a few years, it suddenly changed direction and lost the Jekyll to gain the Hyde. It was quite bizarre, and I couldn't see why it happened. Senior board members hadn't changed that much, and circumstances didn't seem to demand it—we weren't fighting for our lives here. But suddenly laws were being broken—and I do mean laws. Suddenly I found myself working for a crooked and corrupt company. What to do? I turned a blind eye for a while, but eventually I too was asked to participate in the law breaking. It was at that point I left. I kept my honor and reputation and went to work for the opposition, its rival. Once there, I was asked about my old company and what it got up to, but I wouldn't give any information that would allow my new bosses to gain benefit over my old company. I don't know why, but it seemed honorable to sit on what I knew. I was happy to talk about the way they did business, just so long as it didn't spill over into this area of legalities.

A few years later I found myself working for a company that was taken over by my old corrupt bunch. By now the company had been caught, punished, and cleaned up its act. Did I want to work for the company again? Not particularly. But I did have an interview with a senior director who said he was happy to have me on board—"At least you know how to keep your mouth shut," he said. The leopard still seemed a bit spotty to me and I walked.

RULE 46

So, how clean is your industry? Your company? You have to know what you might be asked to do and what is legal and what isn't. Some industries have incredibly minute and trivial laws that you can run foul of almost without realizing it. But realize it you must. To be a Rules Player you have to be cleaner than clean, above suspicion, and never allow yourself to be scapegoated into anything. If your company is looking for a sucker, make sure it ain't you. Make sure you stay clearly this side of the line, and don't stray over it accidentally.

If you choose to break the law, that's one thing, but how awful it would be if you ended up in prison because you didn't know. Better to be an intelligent convict than a stupid one— "But I didn't know" has never been an effective defense.

> ## TO BE A RULES PLAYER YOU HAVE TO BE CLEANER THAN CLEAN.

Set Personal Standards

Do you sleep nights? I know I do, but then I set personal standards that I simply won't break.

- I will not knowingly hurt or hinder another human being in the pursuit of my career.
- I will not knowingly break any laws in the furtherance of my career.
- I will have a moral code that I will follow no matter what.
- I will endeavor to provide a positive contribution to society by what I do for a living.
- I will not do anything that I would be ashamed to talk to my children about.
- I will put my family first at all times.
- I will not work evenings or weekends unless it is an emergency and I have discussed it with my partner.
- I will not unfairly harm anyone in my pursuit of new work.
- I will always endeavor to put something back.
- I will pass on freely and openly any skills, knowledge, or experience to anyone who could use them to benefit themselves within the same industry—I won't hog information for the sake of it.
- I will not be jealous of anyone else's success in the same industry.
- I will question the long-term ramifications of what I do constantly.
- I will play by the Rules at all times.

This code of conduct is my own personal set of standards. It might not suit you. You may need or have a better set. I do hope you don't opt for a worse one. We must endeavor to be the very, very best we can at all times.

> WE MUST ENDEAVOR TO
> BE THE VERY, VERY BEST
> WE CAN AT ALL TIMES.

Never Lie

This Rule, as in the case of *Rule 42: Don't Swear*, is very easy. It sets a limit that you don't have to think about. Never lie means exactly that—never lie. Under no circumstances do you lie. Once you have got a reputation as someone who never lies, you won't ever be asked to cover up, or cover for anyone else.

If you do decide to lie for a living, you have too many choices and decisions. Where do you draw the line? Do you only tell little lies? Great big ones? Do you lie to save yourself? Others? Do you lie for the company? For your boss? For colleagues? How developed will your lies be? Will you add lie to lie when the first lie looks like it's about to be detected? Where will you stop this process? Will you involve other people in your lies? Or will you be a lone liar?

Can you see the problems? If you have a simple Rule—never lie—you have a default setting that requires no thought, no choices, no decisions, no alternatives, no picking, no preferences.

Not ever lying also saves you from guilt, fear, recrimination, having to remember the lies, the risk of being punished or sacked or embarrassed, ostracizing your colleagues, putting your family in jeopardy, running the risk of a criminal prosecution, and not sleeping nights.

Never lie is really the simplest, cleanest, most honest approach to your working life and career.

It is, of course, OK to embellish and hype up your resume or experience or enthusiasm, but please don't actually lie. You will be found out—I guarantee it.

If I'm offering a book to a publisher and they ask me what it is like, I don't say, "It's alright, I suppose." No, instead I say, "It's brilliant, simply brilliant. It will sell extremely well and might well be the best seller we're looking for." Is any of this a lie? Not really. I wouldn't be writing it if I didn't think it was brilliant. Will it sell that well? It might. Who am I to know for certain? It's a changeable market. Is it a lie to say it will? No.

You are allowed to talk up your qualities or skills or expertise—just don't actually tell a lie. And a lie is anything that can be proved definitely to be wrong. To say you are qualified as a software programmer when you aren't is a lie. To say you are a wizard at software programming isn't because it is a matter of opinion rather than fact. But if in doubt—never lie or embellish if you can't think fast on your feet.

> YOU ARE ALLOWED TO
> TALK UP YOUR QUALITIES
> OR SKILLS OR EXPERTISE—
> JUST DON'T ACTUALLY
> TELL A LIE.

RULE 49

Never Cover up for Anyone Else

Being a Rules Player means you are aiming for perfection, that you are setting extremely high standards for yourself. Others will not have these standards—obviously, they won't be as successful as you because of this—but they may well try to either get you to lower yours or to involve you in their shenanigans. What do you do? Again, be happy with a simple default setting—you don't cover up for anyone, ever, under any circumstances.

This way it is simple. You don't have to think about this. You have no choices or decisions to make. You know exactly where you stand. You have let your colleagues know exactly where they stand. You have let your boss know that you won't cover for anyone; therefore you are above suspicion, trustworthy, reliable, beyond reproach.

If you do decide to cover for others, it complicates your life so much that it can't really be worth it. For instance, do you only cover for close colleagues or anyone who asks? Do you only cover for small incidents or the big ones? What about covering for fraud? Criminal negligence? What do you say and do when you get found out? How do you explain it to your family when you get sacked?

How do you handle it when asked to cover up for a close colleague who might well be a friend as well? You can be fairly assertive and just say "No"—you don't have to explain. Or you can soften the blow by saying: "Please don't ask me, I would have to say no if you do," to give them a get-out clause and save their face.

Once you have done this, it gets easier—you've established a reputation for not covering up. The hardest bit is ignoring the emotional blackmail that often accompanies a request to cover up for someone. But in reality that is quite easy to ignore in the sense that if people think so little of you to use this technique, then why the hell shouldn't you turn them down? They have already cooked their goose by using such an approach on you.

If they put pressure on you, adopt the stuck record technique and just keep saying: "No, I can't, please don't ask. No, I can't, please don't ask ...." They'll crack before you. Always remember that real friends will never ask you to cover up for them.

> IF YOU DO DECIDE TO
> COVER FOR OTHERS,
> IT COMPLICATES YOUR
> LIFE SO MUCH THAT
> IT CAN'T REALLY
> BE WORTH IT.

RULE 50

Keep Records

When a publisher and I agree to do a book together, we draw up a contract. This specifies all those things that could get forgotten along the way. That way, when I deliver the manuscript and the publisher says, "But this is only 100 pages and I thought we had agreed on 200," I can produce the contract and find the clause where it clearly states 100 pages, or so many words, or whatever.

If your boss asks you to do something and you make a note of it—in front of him—he will have a very hard job arguing later that you've done it wrong or late.

If you have to submit a report, then drop your boss a quick memo or note outlining the salient facts, very briefly, so there will be no confusion later. Keep a copy. Make sure your boss knows you have kept a copy.

This technique isn't to cover your back because you are up to no good. Instead it clarifies all issues. If it's in writing, it makes your job so much simpler, so much easier. Who can argue with a written memo? In fact, such things could be forged, written afterwards, changed, amended, and/or rewritten, but we all assume they aren't, that they are tamper proof.

It is amazing how often the tiniest detail will cause a major upset—unless you got it in writing in the first place. Keeping records isn't an anal thing to do, but a sensible precaution. None of us has perfect memory. We all forget things—dates, times, details. Once we have made a note of whatever it is, we can refer to it later. And often surprise ourselves with how badly we have remembered something.

RULE 50

You will often read in management books the advice to throw away all memo or emails or faxes over a certain age—if you haven't looked at it in six months then you don't need it. Rubbish. You hang on to everything. Make more filing space rather than throw anything away, unless and until you are 100 percent certain it is not needed. I once had a major quarrel with a publisher (not this one, of course) relating to a book I had written for them five years previously. It was a dispute that wasn't covered by anything in the contract. But I had kept my original notes and could produce them—a bit like having to show your work during math at school—and could show that what they had published had been exactly what they had asked for. I was off the hook. You won't get me throwing anything away. No way.

> IF IT'S IN WRITING,
> IT MAKES YOUR JOB SO
> MUCH SIMPLER,
> SO MUCH EASIER.

RULE 51

Know the Difference Between the Truth and the Whole Truth

While we have ascertained that you ain't never ever gonna lie and you don't cover up for colleagues no matter what, you don't have to be a goody goody and tell tales. You don't need to volunteer information unless it directly helps you to do so. Knowing that a colleague has screwed up doesn't mean you have to run to the boss and rat on him. Instead, it might be beneficial sometimes to stand back and watch how things develop. If your colleague knows you know and you ain't saying anything, there might be a favor being born there that could be recalled later.

And, of course, if you do get asked, you don't lie. But, again, know the difference between the truth and the whole truth. Not lying is one thing, but throwing up and regurgitating everything you do know is something else. Sometimes it pays to be a little editorial with what truth you are giving out. The beauty of being a Rules Player is that you move up and are successful and you are still able to live with yourself—to be a thoroughly nice person. This means you don't lie and don't cover up, but it also means you don't spy on your colleagues, rat on them, betray them, or harm them.

Look, it's a real world out there, and it can be dog eat dog. Be careful—there are some pretty unsavory characters. There may be ruthlessness going on around you, but you don't have to participate. You don't have to be a teacher's pet, either. Keep your wits about you at all times, and know when to spill the beans and when to shut the duck up.

I guess you have to be a diplomat—knowing what to say and when to say it; martial arts expert—thinking on your feet; therapist—letting others bring their problems to you, but keeping yours to yourself; and Zen master—all seeing, all knowing, saying little.

So when people ask for your opinion, you have to weigh up what it is they are really asking. Do they really want the truth? Their report sucks. Or a limited version of the truth? Your report is fine, it'll just about do the job. A highlighted truth? Your report is good but you have missed out quite a lot. A reassurance truth? Your report is really good and I liked it, and I like you because your report is so good. Or the real truth? I haven't had time to read it yet because I don't like you and think it'll be a pretty boring report—bit like you really.

> ## THERE MAY BE RUTHLESSNESS GOING ON AROUND YOU, BUT YOU DON'T HAVE TO PARTICIPATE.

Cultivate Your Support/ Contacts/Friends

If you don't cover up for people, what use are you to them? As I have said, it's a real world out there, and people expect a lot of you. They want you to be in their debt. They want you to carry the can, cover up for them, do their dirty work for them and watch their back—and all at the same time. But you are a Rules Player now, and that takes you outside the spheres of petty office gang warfare. You are now a stand-alone item. You don't feed with the sharks, and yet you avoid being their food. What are you, and what are you for?

You are a pool of calm, the eye of the storm. You are the reliable strength of the team, unshakeable and unshaken. You are the default setting, the honesty factor, the standard by which all other colleagues judge themselves. If you think it's a no-go area then they will know it is. If you turn your back on a tricky situation, they too will know it's not to be touched. If you say it's fine, then they know it's a good thing.

You are the standard bearer, the criterion by which all else is judged. Don't believe me? Try it; it works.

And because you are so reliable, honest, trustworthy, other colleagues will quickly come to rely on you for advice and guidance. You, however, give nothing away for free. Every pat on the back, every prod in the right direction, every session of useful hints and tips, every point of guidance comes with a price—loyalty. You may not hunt with the pack, but by golly the pack had better know who really is pack leader. Yep, you. How to achieve this? By kindness, by consideration, by playing it straight. Never let them down. Never rat on them. Never drop them in it. Always be cheerful, supportive, loyal—don't lie or cover up, but do close ranks if you can—protective, cooperative, caring, and genuinely interested in them as human beings. You'll have 'em eating out of your hand. Why? Because this is a rare game to play. Playing it straight is such an unusual thing that they will have no defense against it, no protection. There are few management training books or courses that teach you to be nice, be straight, be honest. The unspoken wisdom is generally be ruthless, take advantage, dog eat dog. The consequence of this is everyone thinks like a dog and not like a real person. You come along and show them how it really should be and they will follow you any-where, you old dog you.

> PLAYING IT STRAIGHT IS
> SUCH AN UNUSUAL THING
> THAT THEY WILL HAVE NO
> DEFENSE AGAINST IT,
> NO PROTECTION.

Date with Caution

There are those who say that you should never date anyone you work with, on the grounds that it can cause resentment, stress, jealousy, distraction, frustration, and generally damage your work and your reputation. If not when things are going well, then certainly when the relationship is in trouble or finishes.

To some extent I agree with this, and certainly there's no excuse for falling into the bad behavior trap at the office party. If you can't resist getting it together with that tasty colleague from accounts while photocopying your bottoms, best skip the party. At least if you ever want to be taken seriously as a Rules Player.

The trouble is, a simple Rule that says "never date a colleague" would be flawed. If I'd followed that advice, my three oldest children would never have been born, and I'm not advocating anything with that result. You see, many people meet their future partners through work, and you can't ignore that possibility.

So what's the Rules Player to do? Well there is an answer, and it's this. Only allow yourself to get involved in serious relationships at work. Of course, you can't be sure the relationship will last forever, but if it doesn't have a chance, steer clear. Here's a good question to ask yourself—is this person more important to you than the job? If you had to give one of them up, which would it be? If you'd sooner give up the job than the relationship, then go ahead.* Of course, with luck you won't have to give up either.

---

* With the date I mean; no need to hand your notice in before you ask your coworker out.

RULE 53

If you get involved with a colleague, of course you have to be grown up and responsible about it. Set ground Rules for the pair of you to follow so that not only does the relationship not interfere with work, but also your maturity and good sense will be respected by your colleagues and managers. Here are some basic principles to get you started:

- No public displays of affection.
- No huddling together sharing whispered conversations and in-jokes.
- Let your immediate colleagues and managers know; otherwise they'll work out something's going on and won't know what. Then behave as if you weren't going out together.
- Ask for certain tasks to be reallocated if there's a conflict of interest. (This is one reason why your boss needs to know.) For example, you can't sensibly appraise, discipline, or interview each other.

> OF COURSE, YOU CAN'T BE SURE THE RELATIONSHIP WILL LAST FOREVER, BUT IF IT DOESN'T HAVE A CHANCE, STEER CLEAR.

Understand Others' Motives

So what motivates you? We know that you are a Rules Player—honest, diligent, hard working, keen, successful, and self-motivated. You get off on doing a job fabulously well, impressing your bosses, earning the respect of your colleagues and the admiration, and loyalty of your juniors. You go home at night knowing you've done a good day's work and that you've been pleasant to everyone and are a thoroughly nice person. You sleep nights because you haven't harmed anyone or broken any laws or behaved badly in any way. You earn lots, but that isn't your driving force—yours is the need to be the very best, the finest that there is. But what motivates everyone else? Ah, to really get on you will need to understand the motives of others.

Understanding their motives means you have to enter the dark and nebulous world of psychology. What gets others off can be very diverse:

- Power
- Money
- Prestige
- Revenge
- A need to hurt
- A need to be loved

RULE 54

Whatever their motives, I can bet they aren't Rules Players—you lot stand out a mile—aloof, calm, in control, dignified, and sophisticated. Anybody whose motives are need and fear and greed should be treated carefully. You will have to make sure you stay on the right side of them without fawning, that you outmaneuvre them without sinking to their level and without being paranoid. Look around your office now and identify what makes each of your colleagues tick, and do the same for your boss and their boss. Learn to identify their motives, and you will be able to handle them easily. Knowledge is power.

> ANYBODY WHOSE MOTIVES ARE NEED AND FEAR AND GREED SHOULD BE TREATED CAREFULLY.

Assume Everyone Else is Playing by Different Rules

So we know what Rules you are following, but what about other people? What are their standards? What Rule book are they following, what drumbeat do they march to? Chances are they are making it up as they go along. This makes them unpredictable and erratic.

Not everybody will have your high standards of honesty and morality. Obviously, some people are kind and dignified—just like you—and are still able to climb the corporate ladder. But there are equally lots out there whose Rules are suspect.

The Rule book you now have must remain a secret. If you reveal your Rules, you have broken the Rules. If you assume that everyone else is playing by different Rules, you won't go far wrong. You don't have to assume that their Rules are better or worse than yours, merely different. If you assume that their Rules are the same as yours or better, you will be constantly let down, disappointed, disillusioned, saddened, and upset.

If you assume their Rules are worse than yours, you will grow mistrustful, apprehensive, paranoid, suspicious, and sceptical.

Assuming that their Rules are different without assuming what those Rules are keeps you open and receptive, cautious but expectant, approachable but not overly trustful, responsive but not gullible.

It's a bit like being a martial arts exponent:

- You are alert and prepared, but not muscle bound or aggressive
- You remain flexible and fluid and can move like a cat and dodge whatever is thrown your way without ever adopting a belligerent stance
- You are ready for anything by being grounded and centred.

> THE RULE BOOK YOU
> NOW HAVE MUST REMAIN
> A SECRET.
> IF YOU REVEAL YOUR
> RULES, YOU HAVE
> BROKEN THE RULES.

RULE 56

Keep the Faith

There are times when you find yourself in a job where the people around you just aren't Rules Players in any sense. They may be corrupt or dishonest, resistant to change, or obstructive in the way they deal with you. What can you do?

Listen, I know this can be tough, but if you drop your standards, you'll make things worse and not better. You don't have to stay in the job, of course, but I appreciate that sometimes leaving a job isn't that easy, and you may feel you have to stick it out. So, keep the moral high ground and hold firm to what you believe in: decency, integrity, honesty, fair dealing, chivalry, progress. If you don't behave decently, why should anyone else? It may be a slim hope for improvement, but it's all you've got.

I once heard from a reader who was stuck in just such a situation. He was clearly a consummate Rules Player and had steadfastly refused to compromise his standards. He'd worked hard to create cooperative teams and driven through changes that were unwelcome but long overdue. Some of his coworkers were so threatened by this that they accused him of all kinds of corruption and bad behavior to get him sacked. And do you know what? His bosses dismissed these allegations outright. You see, being a Rules Player had paid off, and despite all his problems at work, his managers weren't stupid and recognized a dedicated and loyal worker when they saw one.

So, if you're in a similar situation, you have my sympathy. All I can say is, stick in there. If you let them get to you, or worse still corrupt you into their way of doing things, you won't be able to survive and sleep nights. If no one is flying the flag for decency, that's the last chance gone. Actually though, most people would rather be friendly and decent and honorable and cooperative. They just don't want to be the first to stick their necks out and do it. In a corrupt environment, it's easier to be corrupt. But if you show the courage that others lack, many of them will follow you. Not all of them, of course, but just a few allies will make you feel a whole lot happier and will vindicate your determination to do what's right and play by the Rules no matter what.

> # IF NO ONE IS FLYING THE FLAG FOR DECENCY, THAT'S THE LAST CHANCE GONE.

RULE 57

Put Things in Perspective

When all is said and done, it is only a job. It ain't your health, your love life, your family, your children, your life, or your soul. If, by the way, it is any of these things, then you really have gone badly wrong along the way.

Your job is just a job. Yes, I know you need the money etc., etc. But it is just a job and there are others.

Having a bad day at work shouldn't cause you to

- Lose sleep
- Go hungry
- Lose your sex drive
- Smoke more
- Drink more
- Take drugs
- Be more irritable
- Get depressed
- Get stressed

But you'd be surprised how often these things are done by people because they have had a bad day. Yes, they may have had a whole series of bad days. But taken one by one, it is just a bad day. You have to learn to switch off, relax, not take it so seriously, enjoy it more, put things into perspective.

RULE 57

Get a hobby, get a life. You must work to live, not live to work. Don't take stuff home with you—learn to be assertive and say no. Put your family first. Spend time with your children—they will grow up so fast you will miss their precious childhood if you work your way through it—believe me, I have seen my children grow up, and it is so swift it is terrifying. It may seem slow and stressful at the time, but it zips past and then is irrecoverably gone—and you missed it because you were doing paperwork one evening or attending another boring conference over the weekend.

It is just a job.

> YOU HAVE TO LEARN TO
> SWITCH OFF, RELAX, NOT
> TAKE IT SO SERIOUSLY,
> ENJOY IT MORE,
> PUT THINGS INTO
> PERSPECTIVE.

PART VI

BLEND IN

No one likes a black sheep or a white crow or a fish that swims in a different direction from the rest of the shoal. These Rules teach you how to blend in, become "one of them" so you don't stand out as an outsider. You might stand out as being the leader of the pack—better, more efficient—but you'll still be "one of us" because you know how to play the "blending in" game.

RULE 58

Know the Corporate Culture

Every corporation, company, industry, or even small office has a culture. Knowing what that culture is gives you the edge, the key to success. Knowledge is power.

The culture is how their people do things. This culture is sometimes company led, but mostly people generated—it grows organically and without plan or strategy. If you don't know this culture—or fail to make use of it—you can end up looking foolish and are then easy to take advantage of, or be belittled.

Bear in mind that around 70 percent of all dismissals are not because someone couldn't do their job properly, but because they didn't know the corporate culture—they didn't fit in.

Consider this advert for a pretty big prestigious design studio—the BMD. When Bruce Mau, the owner of this company, wanted to recruit new staff, he put out a quiz with some 40 questions, including, "Who made a film consisting of nothing but the color blue?"*

Bruce headed the advert, "Avoid fields. Jump fences." As a result of this, he lured some of the best, most talented top designers to come and work for him—or with him, as he describes his working relationship with his staff.

Now what sort of corporate culture do you think Bruce expects, wants, gets? How would you fit in? What do you think Bruce would expect of you?

---

* By the way, it was Derek Jarman, of course.

You don't have to buy into the corporate culture—you don't have to believe in it—all you have to do is fit in. If they all play golf, then you play golf. I know you hate golf, but you will play golf—if that's what it takes to fit in. Now you may, of course, question whether you want to fit in. You may question whether playing golf is where you want to be. But if you are a Rules Player and you want to move up and be successful and you also want to be part of a particular company where playing golf is the corporate culture—then play it you must.

> YOU DON'T HAVE TO BUY INTO THE CORPORATE CULTURE—YOU DON'T HAVE TO BELIEVE IN IT— ALL YOU HAVE TO DO IS FIT IN.

Speak the Language

Fitting in means being able to follow the corporate culture, and speaking the language is a big part of this. You can give the game away by not using the right jargon or using computer-speak at the wrong time. If they all use geeky language, then you too must use it. No, this isn't the time or place to discuss whether you want to belong to a geeky company—that's for you to do alone in the soul-searching time of the early hours when you can't sleep.

If the boss talks in terms of SPRs for staff product ratios, then you too must talk of SPRs. It isn't your job to educate them, re-educate them, edify them, inform them, teach them, give them a bit of class, drag them up, stop the dumbing-down process, or instruct them. Their corporate language is what you must speak. I know there will be times when it will make you want to scream—but speak it you must.

I once worked for an Italian boss who, because of his inadequate grasp of English, had taken to talking of "clienters," which was his sort of mix of clients and customers. Because he was the boss, this ridiculous term had entered the public domain, and every member of staff from the general manager down talked about the clienters. I could have stood there and screamed, "No, no, no, this is wrong, stop it at once." Fat lot of good it would have done me. It was clienters the whole time I was there, and I hated it every time I heard it. But I knew the Rules and also called them clienters.

Spend a little time listening to how your office uses language. We're not talking accents here, but the sort of individual clienters that every office somehow manages to pick up. I also worked with a guy who talked of people working as hard as Mexicans. This was his way of being, what he thought, politically correct. It was, of course, just as bad, just as wrong, just as offensive. However, he was the owner of the company, so the term "Mexicans" had stuck and, again, it was wrong and horrible, but it was in current usage.

The only time this Rule should be broken is where it applies to swearing. The Rules say no swearing, but if the corporate culture is that everyone swears, what are you to do? Answer: not swear. *Rule 42* over-rules *Rule 59* in this case—you've been trumped.

> IF THEY ALL USE GEEKY
> LANGUAGE, THEN YOU
> TOO MUST USE IT.

RULE 60

Dress Up or Down Accordingly

You will always dress elegantly, stylishly, smartly. But what if you work for a design company where they all wear jeans and a T-shirt? In that case, you will wear jeans too. Just make sure your jeans are the smartest, the most stylish, the most fashionable, the most modern—no, no, you do not iron them! No creases, for God's sake!

Watch what the others do. If, at a meeting, it is jackets off and sleeves rolled up, then that's what you do. If it is very formal and jackets stay on, then yours stays on as well. I know this may sound obvious, but you would be surprised how often you look around a meeting and you can see the one person marching to a different drumbeat—and that's the one who will be ostracized by the others.

To a greater or lesser extent, we all need to belong to the herd, to fit in, to blend in, to camouflage ourselves so we don't draw unnecessary attention to ourselves. Obviously, if it is the boss who takes their jacket off, then you too do so. Don't become a clone though and mindlessly follow what everyone else is doing. We are talking here of dressing up or down on a general basis, not each and every minute.

I've always found it better to sit back for a moment or two to see what others do rather than to be the first to follow the head lemming. Stand back for a moment, it might be a cliff and not a promotion opportunity; or a springboard with no water below.

RULE 60

I've always found it useful to have a role model to check with to see if they would have done a certain thing or worn a certain style of dress. For a lot of my business life I've used Cary Grant. Easy then to ask, "Would Cary have worn this?" If the answer is yes, then go right ahead. If the answer is no, then don't. See how easy this is? Try Humphrey Bogart, but in *Casablanca* rather than *The African Queen*.

Even if the corporate culture is to dress casual, you can still make an effort.

> TO A GREATER OR LESSER
> EXTENT, WE ALL NEED TO
> BELONG TO THE HERD.

RULE 61

Be Adaptable in Your Dealings with Different People

Being a chameleon is a good thing just so long as you can carry it off. People are all different, and if you try to treat them all the same you run the risk of offending them all or at least failing to satisfy any of them.

It is a lot easier to understand this Rule if you are a parent. If you have more than one child, you will know how essential it is not to treat them the same. Each child needs different motivating forces. For some it is enough to be mildly disappointed. For others you have to be a real ogre just to get them to get dressed in the morning.

I have five sons and a daughter, and I have to treat each one differently. Sometimes I forget and treat them all the same, and they are quite surprised and quite hurt. Each needs me to be something different, something unique for them, something special. As a manager, you are a sort of parent to your people and must treat them as individuals.

I once staged a completely fake loss of temper to get my own way over a fairly trivial matter. The person for whose benefit the tantrum was put on was so shocked that I was given into immediately. Now there are quite a few bosses around for whom such behavior would have been intolerable, and I would have been shown the door straightaway.

When I was a general manager I always felt I could get the best out of my workforce by being fairly pleasant and quite kind. But there were the odd few who didn't respond to this type of behavior. They were so entrenched in their old-fashioned approach to work that they expected a boss to be a complete bastard and to shout at them and tell them what to do. And here I was asking them how they were and what they thought of it all. They couldn't cope, and I had to be unpleasant to them to get them to respond—different strokes for different folks.

You have to be adaptable, ready to change quickly depending on what is required of you. The perfect manager is the one with the ability to spin on a dime. Study how you are with people. Are you always the same, no matter who they are or what is going on? Do you adapt and change readily and easily? Identify who around you is successful, and watch what they do with people.

> THE PERFECT MANAGER
> IS THE ONE WITH THE
> ABILITY TO SPIN ON
> A DIME.

RULE 62

Make Your Boss Look Good

If your boss looks good, your department looks good. And that reflects well on you. So this one should be obvious. But I'm amazed at how many people criticize the boss behind her back, or are always ready to pass the buck on to her.

I realize that your boss may be a fool, have no business acumen, be difficult and demanding, have abysmal people skills, no idea how to manage a department, and lack all integrity, talent, and diplomacy. If all that is true, her image certainly needs all the help you can give it.

OK, few bosses are that bad. But few are faultless either, and that's not the point. It's just common sense. You benefit all round from making your boss look good, and it's only a matter of time before your boss starts to notice.

Of course, this makes sense when your boss is present, but if you stick up for her, give her credit and draw attention to her strengths even when she's not there, it will do you even more good. Other senior managers will be impressed, and word will get back to the boss about how you told everyone it was your boss's thoroughness that kept the exhibition stand on budget, or she who negotiated that great deal, or her encouragement that gave the team the confidence to give such a good presentation.

This is the kind of loyalty that other managers will admire and will help consolidate the rest of your department into a strong team—which will also be noticed and will rub off on everyone, yourself included. I'm not suggesting here that you lie about the boss if she in fact makes a complete mess of things.

I'm suggesting that you keep quiet on the subject if she really screwed up, and make a noise about the stuff she gets right.

Of course, there will be times when you and your colleagues need to discuss the boss honestly to work as a team, but make sure you make only those negative points that are strictly necessary, and be fair and impersonal about them. It's probably wise to acknowledge that your boss is likely to give you the information you need at the last possible minute, but you can still voice it in a matter-of-fact practical way rather than a bitchy, critical way.

> THIS IS THE KIND OF LOYALTY THAT OTHER MANAGERS WILL ADMIRE.

RULE 63

Know Where to Hang Out, and When

There are always key places where the high and mighty gather at formal and informal times. You need to check these places out and use them, as important places to garner information, make contacts, be seen, and make an impact. Outside work there will be a watering hole used by senior bosses. It might be the golf club 19th hole, the local bar, a certain restaurant, a club. Whatever, wherever. It is your duty to know where this is. Now don't go rushing in there and make a complete idiot of yourself. You have to spy out the land, learn the territory so as to be informed of everything you need to know before going in. Does the restaurant have a dress code or style you should know about? Is there a waiting list for membership of the golf club? Is the bar the sort of place you'd go alone, or should you go with your partner? Is the club easy to join? Can you just hang out with the bosses without looking out of place? Are these places the sort you could just happen to be there,—"I was just passing"—or will it be obvious that you are hanging around waiting to make a move?

You have to be careful with this one, but you should know where they meet and the accessibility of such places. Chances are you might choose never to go there. That's fine. But if it crops up in conversation, you will have an edge just knowing where they go—knowledge is power.

At work there may be a corridor where they hang out next to the coffee machine or photocopier. You can always make sure you happen to be passing. Get your face known; get your name known.

At formal occasions perhaps the bosses all go out for a smoke. Even if you don't indulge, you can still pop out and be part of that smoking gang. Or maybe they all like to visit the bar before going into the conference or whatever. Make sure you are there first so you don't have to have an excuse for dropping in.

> GET YOUR FACE KNOWN;
> GET YOUR NAME KNOWN.

RULE 64

Understand the Social Protocols

Within every company and place of work there will be social protocols. Know them and use them. They might be quite simple:

- You never take partners to the staff dinner.
- You always turn up for the staff meetings on your days off.
- You never park in a certain couple of spaces even though they aren't marked because they are unofficially reserved for the CEO's partner and kids.
- You always give a $5 to the leaving envelopes that go round but only a couple of dollars for the birthdays.
- You never take the jelly doughnut with the coffee because that's Sylvia's—always has been, always will be.
- You always refer to the CEO as Charles to his face but as Charlie to the rest of the staff.
- It is OK to order wine with lunch, but beer really is frowned on.

You may never know where some of these unwritten Rules come from—Charles once got hit by a beer drinking employee, hence no beer at lunch; Charles was once embarrassed by the wife of a junior manager who made a not completely unsuccessful pass at him at a staff dinner, hence no partners.

Of course, these social protocols may be obvious—Sylvia likes the jelly doughnuts and she has the clout to get her own way—the important thing is to identify them, file them away if you like, but by golly you'd better know them if you don't want to make any terrible social gaffes.

I once worked for a company where it was considered taboo to drink during a working day in any way. You couldn't even have a beer at lunch. Alcohol was a big no-no and I couldn't find out why. I was happy to go along with this, as I am not a drinker, but it puzzled me. I eventually found out that the company had had a finance manager who had spent every afternoon having 40 winks in his office—sleeping it off. In fact, he wasn't. He did drink a lot every lunchtime, but the afternoons were spent carefully siphoning off funds to his own accounts. He was eventually caught and dismissed, but after that no drinking was the Rule—and no closed office doors.

> OF COURSE, THESE
> SOCIAL PROTOCOLS MAY
> BE OBVIOUS—THE
> IMPORTANT THING IS
> TO IDENTIFY THEM,
> FILE THEM AWAY.

RULE 65

Know the Rules About Authority

Who runs your office? I bet it ain't the boss. Bosses tend to closet themselves away in their ivory office, leaving the real job of running the business to someone else. Your job is to identify this person and stay on the right side of them.

I have worked for companies where the real power resided in the hands of a PR consultant, a legal secretary, an auditor, a customer, and a junior manager. In each and every case, the reason why they were really in charge was that they

- Had the ear of the boss
- Were trusted by the boss
- Carried out a subtle whispering campaign rather than saying anything outright or up front
- Had been there quite some time
- Were motivated entirely by power and control
- Were invariably unpleasant enough to use various tactics to get their own way—no matter what
- Were extremely clever, but lacking the experience, qualifications, or skill to actually do the job properly

In each case, once I had made a friend of these people I got on better. To begin with, I didn't spot them immediately. This always caused me problems. I would go to the boss and only later be made to realize I had committed a gaffe by doing so— "Oh everything goes through Sarah first," "I'll just run it by Janine first to see if she thinks it a good idea," "Do you want to check this out with Trevor and come back to me?"

I soon learned to go to the person who had the ear of the boss first. Play the game with this person, and don't make an enemy of her. She is the real authority, and you should pay her homage. I know it ain't fair and you hate it, but until a better system comes along, we have to work with what we've got.

> WHO RUNS YOUR OFFICE?
> I BET IT AIN'T THE BOSS.

Know the Rules About the Office Hierarchy

This Rule goes hand in hand with the previous one. You have to know who has the boss's ear, and you have to know who runs the office. You might be quite senior, but you won't get the key to the stationery cupboard no matter what, not unless you speak nicely to Mark first. And your morning coffee is going to be delivered cold if you upset the catering staff at all by wandering up to the break room and ordering your coffee without going through the office manager first.

Office protocols and hierarchies are old fashioned, petty, small minded, outdated, and yet still very much with us. It wasn't that long ago that I worked in an office where you had to take your typing to an office manager who then handed it to a typist and it was returned to you later, all done.

Trouble was that if you upset the office manager—and you could do this by smoking near her, talking about the boss in a derogatory way, swearing, coming to work causally dressed— you got your work given to the worst typist and it came back late, full of mistakes, coffee cup stained, misspelled, no copies, you name it.

Once you got on the right side of the office manager, it all changed and your typist presented you with exemplary work, on time and immaculate.

Now, you might say that this was the way it was and I couldn't really complain. Yes, but the office manager wasn't my office manager. I only used the typing facility occasionally and I was senior. I still had to go through this hierarchy, which involved me in having to seek the patronage of someone junior to get a fairly mundane and routine job done. It sure made me mad, and I had to spend quite a lot of time wooing the office manager just to get a letter done. It was time consuming, unproductive, and petty. But you're right—we have to work with what we've got.

So what do we do? We play the game. We have no choice but to smile and woo them.

OFFICE PROTOCOLS AND HIERARCHIES ARE OLD FASHIONED, PETTY, SMALL MINDED, OUTDATED, AND YET STILL VERY MUCH WITH US.

RULE 67

Never Disapprove of Others

So, they're all going to the wine bar again this lunchtime. You hate that. You hate the noise, the smell, the inane chatter about last night's TV programs.

But do you tell them this? No, you do not. You need to be one of the crowd—blend in. You need them to think you're there, in spirit if not in body, without actually being there. Easy. You get out of it by saying you have to do some shopping, visit a friend, go to the gym.

Don't disapprove of the way they spend their lunch break— this will make them think of you as an outsider. Nor do you tell them you're staying in the office to catch up on some work—they will think you a creep. But it is fine to say you are going to do some shopping and then find somewhere nice to park in your car with a soft drink and a decent sandwich—and your laptop. You can get all that extra work done, but you don't have to let them know.

Don't tell them that you think drinking at lunchtime is unhealthy and unproductive—tell them you'll be along in a bit and to carry on without you—"get one in for me." This way the lunchtime crowd will accept you as "one of them" without your ever having to be one. You will be accepted if you don't disapprove.

Or perhaps they all go bowling together on a Tuesday evening. No, you don't say "but bowling is for geeks, isn't it?" Instead you can say, "Ah, Tuesday evenings? That's my night for taking my mother to the cinema, I'm afraid." Or how about you swallow your pride, your standards, and your disapproval—and actually go. Who knows, maybe you'll have fun. But you will blend in and you won't show that you disapprove of your colleagues. Smart move.

How others spend their leisure time, their money, or their lives is no concern of yours. Smart movers concentrate on their own path and ignore the route others choose to take. Keep focused on where you are going, and ignore anything others are up to. By ignoring, it is easier to stop making judgments. If you make judgments, you categorize yourself and thus make it much more difficult to be flexible and to move easily from situation to situation. By judging others you, in turn, get pigeon-holed yourself—not a good place to be.

> SMART MOVERS
> CONCENTRATE ON THEIR
> OWN PATH AND IGNORE
> THE ROUTE OTHERS
> CHOOSE TO TAKE.

RULE 68

Understand the Herd Mentality

People like to form nice safe little groups—family, friends, work colleagues, town, country, nation, regiment—and will fight quite fiercely to protect these groups. If you threaten them—or, and this is important, are thought to threaten them—they won't like it. So don't. Understand that this herd mentality is important and that to blend in is important.

Suppose your herd is a pride of lions. Yes, you can roll in the dust, roar, eat zebras, and be very fierce and you will blend in—you will be a lion. This doesn't mean you have to capitulate though or be weak. In every pride there is a top dog—a senior lion. You can blend in but still stand out by being in charge, being a pack leader, being the head honcho.

Blending in is about being a chameleon, not a wimp. Just because I say you ought to blend in doesn't mean you have to give up your identity or become a clone or lose all sense of your individuality. All you have to do is know and understand herd mentality—and then use it to your own advantage. I once saw an employee reduced to tears because he didn't know the system and the herd—his fellow workers—turned on him. He was "different," and they smelled his fear and went for him.

What you are going to be is the proverbial wolf in sheep's clothing. If the sheep accept you, then you can do pretty much what you want with them. If they detect any whiff of wolfishness, they start to get very unsettled.

RULE 68

Study any group of people and you will see conformity. They all like to be sheep; it makes them feel

- Secure
- Comfortable
- Safe
- Protected.

All their thinking has been done for them and they can just eat grass cozy and safe in the knowledge that they will be taken care of. You don't need these things; they're for the sheep. You are the wolf. Think independent, wolfish thoughts.

> THINK INDEPENDENT,
> WOLFISH THOUGHTS.

PART VII

ACT
ONE STEP
AHEAD

If you are going to move on up, you had better start practicing now. These Rules teach you how to adopt the mannerisms, attitudes, and managerial traits of the position above the one you currently hold. If you already look as if you've been promoted, chances are you will be.

RULE 69

Dress One Step Ahead

When I was an assistant manager, I dressed like one. When I wanted to be a manager, I studied what managers wore—and general managers. I opted to dress like a general manager and was duly promoted, thus missing out on the manager's position in between assistant and general. There is a style for every job. You may choose the job you want. Now you can choose to dress like that job. Then you will get that job. It is that simple. Just so long as when you get that job you can do that job—don't fly until you can crawl.

I have held many interviews in my time for many different positions to be filled. I have never ceased to be amazed at how people dress for interviews. It's almost as if they don't want the job. I've seen interviewees for senior management positions turn up in a crumpled suit, an unironed shirt or blouse, unpolished shoes, and uncombed hair. I wouldn't employ them as—here I have to be careful as I don't want to insult any group of workers—ferret catchers.

I've seen interviews, again for senior management posts, where they turned up late, in the wrong place, on the wrong day, with the wrong information, and obviously for the wrong job.

I've held interviews for trainees where they turned up in tennis shoes—not quite what I had in mind.

Whatever job you are doing, you must have your eye on the next position up. Haven't you? If you have your eye on that job, you must know who has that job now. Study that person. What does he wear? How does he dress? What style, level of smartness? Is there anything you could learn from the way this person dresses? Can you start copying it now? And when I say copying it, I do mean learning to dress like that for real. If it means wearing a smart business suit, then get used to it.

There's nothing worse than starting a new job and starting to wear a new style at the same time. It will be noticed that the collar doesn't fit or the shoes seem too tight or strange, and that the level of smartness is all wrong for you—you're always pulling the hem of your skirt down or straightening that tie that feels so strange to you.

> YOU MAY CHOOSE THE JOB
> YOU WANT. NOW YOU CAN
> CHOOSE TO DRESS LIKE
> THAT JOB. THEN YOU WILL
> GET THAT JOB.

RULE 70

Talk One Step Ahead

How does your boss talk? I assume it is her job you want. If it ain't, whose job is it? Or have I been wasting my time here? Come on, whose job do you want? Let's start with the boss. How does your boss talk?

What do I mean—how does your boss talk? I'll explain. It isn't her accent or pronunciation—how she sounds—but the content, what she says. I bet you talk in terms of "I," whereas your boss will probably use "we" much more. You might speak from a worker's point of view, whereas your boss will speak on behalf of the company.

The more senior you go, the less likely you are to

- Chatter inanely
- Gossip
- Swear
- Talk about last night's TV programs or any other issues that have no relevance to the work being done—bosses tend to be much more focused and less inclined to waste time
- Prattle on—bosses tend to be more thoughtful and pause before speaking (or at least the good ones do)

So, if you are going to talk one step up, you need to be more thoughtful, talk about issues that are relevant, talk in terms of "we" rather than "I," be focused and dynamic, and keep personal details to yourself—bosses don't chatter or gossip about their social lives.

I guess what you have to do is be the grown-up and speak to the other workers as children. You become aloof and slightly withdrawn, mature and responsible, dependable and conscientious.

When I say aloof I do not mean arrogant. I'm sure you have encountered lots of managers who make this simple mistake. Arrogance has no place at work. Arrogance is conceit and fake importance. Aloofness is being slightly withdrawn, being detached, being superior by nature of experience, skill, and natural ability.

> BE FOCUSED AND DYNAMIC, AND KEEP PERSONAL DETAILS TO YOURSELF—BOSSES DON'T CHATTER OR GOSSIP ABOUT THEIR SOCIAL LIVES.

RULE 71

Act One Step Ahead

So, we've got you dressing one step up and talking one step up; now you have to act one step up. I know, I know, it's all too much, too hard, too difficult. Who said this was going to be easy? Not me, pal. I told you right from the word go that this was going to be hard—harder in fact than just doing the job like normal people. Being a Rules Player takes more effort, requires more attention to detail, and is generally more like hard work than hard work. But the results are fantastic. In fact, being a Rules Player automatically qualifies you for promotion—if you can be a Rules Player you deserve to be promoted. It's a sort of self-fulfilling prophecy. Carrying out the Rules requires strength of character, will power, determination, honesty, courage, experience, great talent, dedication, drive, nerve, and charisma—if you've got all these, you'll be promoted anyway.

So, act one step up. Look at the way your boss enters the office. Notice anything? Watch the way he answers the phone, talks to staff, entertains customers, holds his pen, hangs up his coat, opens his office door, sits down, stands up—anything he does. I bet you'll notice that he moves differently from, say, the office manager or the maintenance team or the sales force or the marketing folk or the PR people.

Acting one step up requires you to

- Be more certain of yourself
- Be more mature
- Be more confident

You have to be languid and suave and sophisticated—no, no, not swaggering or aggressive. A simple exercise—do you have your own office? Do people knock on your door? What do you say? A mild "Come in, please"? or a one-step-up "Come." The higher you go, the less time you have to waste. You get slicker and quicker, sleeker and fitter. You don't have time to waffle or use long expressions—a simple "Come" is more expedient. You too have to be expedient. That's the secret. Next.

CARRYING OUT THE RULES
REQUIRES STRENGTH OF
CHARACTER, WILL POWER,
DETERMINATION,
HONESTY, COURAGE,
EXPERIENCE, GREAT
TALENT, DEDICATION,
DRIVE, NERVE, AND
CHARISMA

RULE 72

Think One Step Ahead

We talked about being expedient. Thinking one step up is about thinking expediently. You don't have time to waste thinking

- How will this affect my coffee breaks?
- Will this mean I can still have my vacations?
- Will I have to work harder? Longer?
- Will I score any kudos from this?
- No, instead you will think
- Is this better for the department?
- Will the company do well from this?
- Can we bosses sell this to the workforce?
- Are our customers going to be happy with this?

Get the message? See the point? You will start to think like a boss and less like a worker. You will see things from the company's point of view and not how it affects your own personal petty little desk footprint:

- See the big picture
- See the entire picture
- Picture the picture
- Direct the picture
- Produce the picture
- Stop being an extra

RULE 72

I guess these Rules teach you how to be an individual, how to think for yourself, how to stand on your own two feet. But if you could do all that you wouldn't need these Rules. And if you can't, can these Rules teach you? Yes, of course they can. Read on.

> YOU WILL START TO THINK
> LIKE A BOSS AND LESS
> LIKE A WORKER.

Address Corporate Issues and Problems

We talked about looking at things from the company's point of view and not from your own. You have to take this further and talk only about corporate issues and problems even when you are talking to yourself or close colleagues. You have to convince them you are already a boss—see *Rule 78*.

I remember doing my first book and naturally being terribly concerned with the look of it—did the cover look right, feel right, smell right? The marketing manager, obviously getting fed up with the interminable dreary phone calls from me to check up on every little detail, finally said, "Tins of beans, dear boy, tins of beans." I didn't know what he meant, and he had to explain it all in words of one syllable. Each book is a product—a tin of beans—it sits on a shelf and gets bought or not bought depending on factors over which I, the mere little writer, have no control—such as the position of the book on the shelves, the competition stationed nearby, the weather, any discounts the bookstore happens to be offering, and on and on and on. All of these things, including fascinating things, such as the color of the cover, can affect sales. It was my job to supply the text and then to start thinking about the corporate issues, such as how many tins of beans get sold in any accounting period, what my percentage share of any tin of beans is, what the next tin of beans will be, and can we sell them spaghetti next time?

When problems crop up, it is easy to see things from your own point of view—how it directly affects you. Once you make the leap to corporate speak, it gets easier to stop doing this and to start seeing problems from the company's point of view. This doesn't mean you have to become a company person hook, line and sinker. In fact, you are allowed to be honest and express your opinion. If it stinks it stinks—and you should say so. But say so from the company's point of view and not your own.

If the company suggests a new procedure, immediately think how it affects your customers and not you.

> IF THE COMPANY SUGGESTS A NEW PROCEDURE, IMMEDIATELY THINK HOW IT AFFECTS YOUR CUSTOMERS AND NOT YOU.

RULE 74

Make Your Company Better for Having You There

One of the most satisfying ways to make your name in an organization is to propose a change that will benefit everyone, not just your own job or even your department.

I'll give you an example. I worked in a company that had one of those suggestion boxes that most people thought was a bit of a pointless exercise, and we didn't believe anyone would take any notice of the suggestions anyway. Until this woman we hardly knew made a blindingly simple suggestion via the box. She recommended that all letters should be sent by second class post as standard, unless there was a good reason to upgrade it to first class. Up until then all post had gone first class.

This was exactly the sort of thing I'm talking about, for several reasons:

- It was incredibly straightforward and required no complex explanations.
- It could be put into practice by everyone in the organization at no cost.
- It was easy to implement.
- It saved the company a lot of money.

That's what you're looking for, ideally. Simple, universal, and of clear and immediate benefit. You can imagine how envious the rest of us were when this previously insignificant employee was the focus of managerial praise and recognition. And deservedly so.

So take a good look at your own job, and see if you can find anything that will benefit everyone—maybe you can see a way to do something cheaper, quicker, or better. Or perhaps you have (or can cultivate) a resource that everyone can use. This is an extension of Rule 4 actually, but this time you're finding something that benefits your colleagues too. Such as collecting lots of disparate information into one place so people can access it more easily. Or writing up a proper user manual for the phone system that every department can use to train new staff.

I'm sure you're getting the message: that if you look for ways to create assets for everyone to share, the credit will rub off on you every time they're used. And that's what it's all about. Genuinely helping everyone, and yourself most of all.

> CAN YOU SEE A WAY TO DO
> SOMETHING CHEAPER,
> QUICKER, OR BETTER?

Talk of "We" Rather Than "I"

I once worked for a boss who asked who we worked for. We said:

- Ourselves
- Our families
- Our bank managers
- Our self-esteem
- Our boss
- The management
- The company board of directors
- The customers
- The inland revenue
- The government

He said a polite "No" to all of these. He explained we worked for the shareholders. That's it. That's who you work for. Now go and buy some of your company's shares. Now you work for yourself. Now you can start to say "we" and "us" instead of "me" and "I" and that sort of thing.

You are now a shareholder, so when you have to talk about company procedure, you can think how it will affect us, the shareholders—and not them, the staff (of whom you used to be one, not so very long ago).

If you go to meetings it is so much more grown up (and cool) to talk of "we" instead of "I."

"If we are going to implement this new procedure, we need to appraise the junior staff's reaction first," instead of "I think this sucks."

"We ought to prioritize some time for talking about the exhibition"—instead of "I'm panicking, this exhibition is only two weeks away and I've done nothing."

> IF YOU GO TO MEETINGS IT IS SO MUCH MORE GROWN UP (AND COOL) TO TALK OF "WE" INSTEAD OF "I."

RULE 76

Walk the Walk

Now you've got to put the whole package together—you've got to walk the walk. You've got to become whoever and whatever it is you aspire to be. This isn't mimicry but training. If you can't walk the walk, you can't do the job.

Remember though what we said right from the outset—you have to be able to come up with the goods, you must be able to do the job, and do it well. That is the bottom line. If you can't do the job, leave the stage.

These Rules are not for the bullshitters or the posers. They are for the really industrious, the talented, the hard working, the naturally gifted, those who are prepared to put in some effort and burn some oil.

Study the job that you aspire to. Who is doing it now? Learn to think of her as the person who is doing your job. How is she handling it? Learn to appraise those who are senior to you in the way that they appraise you. Don't moan or whine about how your boss does the job—observe instead her mistakes and learn and profit from them. Watch where she goes wrong and swear never to make the same mistakes. Watch what she does superbly well and start practicing her smart moves now.

If you are going to walk your walk, you have to have the right mannerisms, the right dress code, the right way of speaking, the right way of acting, the right responses, and the right attitude. You only get these if you are prepared to put in some time carrying out a four-point plan:

- Watching
- Learning
- Practicing
- Incorporating

If you are prepared to do these four things, you will fly. Of course, you also have to do these without anyone knowing what you are doing—as well as doing your normal everyday job. Tough order? Of course. Who said it was going to be easy?

> YOU'VE GOT TO BECOME
> WHOEVER AND WHATEVER
> IT IS YOU ASPIRE TO BE.

RULE 77

Spend More Time with Senior Staff

No matter what level you are in the company, you can spend time with senior members of staff and they won't even realize it if you handle it right. Draw attention to yourself, and you will be spotted as an interloper, a spy, an intruder, a gate-crasher. Remember as a small child you could attend grown-up parties if you stayed quiet. They forgot you were there. Once spotted, you got carried off to bed—where you belonged. It's the same as a junior. You can hang around and learn, but don't blow it or you'll be sent back to bed metaphorically.

When I was an office junior I noticed that senior members of staff tended to hang back after meetings sort of chewing the fat among themselves. The juniors scuttled off leaving these bigwigs to chat. I found that if I hung around also, sort of tidying up the table, emptying ashtrays (those were the days) and keeping quiet, then I got to overhear a lot and was even consulted on the odd occasion—"Ah, Richard, you're part of the new invoicing procedures, what do you think of them?" This was my chance to shine. I blew it, of course, and stammered and blushed and was tongue tied and useless. Next time I got it better and eventually got it right.

There came a time when I was asked something and I was coherent, confident and mature. Strange that I was also whisked up the promotion ladder quite rapidly very soon after. This was when I was working for a very old-fashioned British company and their promotion route was very fixed; you had to follow a very set procedure. I was allowed to bypass this system, and I put it all down to hanging around the top guns.

Sometimes you will notice a boss sitting on his own at a lunch or social occasion. Most "workers" are too nervous to go up to bosses and chat or so entrenched in their social class thing that they can't talk to them. Forget that. Go up and make small talk. You'll be amazed how often bosses are grateful for a "worker" talking to them because they too are human and feel isolated, lonely, ignored, forgotten. They are glad for a chat, just so long as you don't take advantage and ask about a pay rise or time off or your vacation. But it is OK to ask about their experiences—"So how did you get into marketing, Ms. Johnson?"

You may well find you pick up useful hints and tips as well as getting ready for the next Rule—getting people to assume you have already made the step.

> YOU'LL BE AMAZED HOW OFTEN BOSSES ARE GRATEFUL FOR A "WORKER" TALKING TO THEM.

Get People to Assume You Have Already Made the Step

Act like a general manager, and people will accept you as one. Act like an office junior, and that's what people will think you are. So how are we going to get people to make this assumption?

- Be confident and assertive and sound mature: "Yes, we can do that—I'll make sure we get on to that immediately."

- Dress the part. If you come to work wearing tennis shoes and sweats, you won't command the same respect as you would if you wore a smart business suit and looked the part.

- Speak of "we." Don't talk of "I" and refer every problem back to how it affects you—"I can't work through my lunch break, I'm entitled to my hour off"—instead of "We" and seeing things from the company's point of view, what's best for the whole organization—"We need to pull together here. I'm happy to work through the lunch break to help us get this problem solved."

- Talk about the business. If you talk about what you watched on TV last night and where you are going on vacation and what you are going to do over the weekend, you come across as more lightweight—and thus junior— than if you talk about company issues, what your department's plans are for the future, how the rise in interest rates is going to affect business over the next few months, and what you are going to do about exchange rates and the euro.

RULE 78

Basically, what you have to do is get people to recognize you as a heavyweight and not a lightweight. Be serious, mature, grown-up, and adult. This doesn't mean you have to be a geek, a nerd, a goody-goody, or a bore. You can still take a joke, enjoy a laugh, smile, be lighthearted and jovial, be fun and full of beans. You need to project a mature but fun image. You need to make people aware that you

- Know the job
- Are experienced
- Are serious
- Are reliable and responsible
- Are trustworthy
- Are the job you want to be

So, take to sauntering around the place looking suave and cool and being very stylish and grown-up, make the appropriate noises and make sure that when you get offered the job you are after, you can already do it.

> ## BE SERIOUS, MATURE, GROWN-UP, AND ADULT.

RULE 79

Prepare for the Step After Next

Sorry, but you can't coast. You are a Rules Player now, and you must stick with it—no days off, no rests, no breaks, no putting your feet up drinking coffee and staring into space. Back to the grindstone. So, you've got your eye on the next step, the next job. Fine, good. But what about after that? What's your next step? What's your next target?

Even before you've got your next promotion, you should already be practicing for the next step. Because if you aren't getting ready now, when will you be? There is always an opportunity to miss a step out, to skip over a promotion if you play this game well. I'm not suggesting this should always be your aim, but be prepared just in case it happens.

Of course, you have your long- and short-term plans—so you will have plotted your career path and know the steps you have to take on your great journey. Even now you will be getting people to assume you have already made the next step, acting the part of the next step, walking your walk, and talking as if you were already the boss, but it doesn't hurt to start practicing for the step after that.

Letting people see that you are officer material is no bad thing. Once people get in the habit of assuming you are a high flier, you become one. If you dress down, talk trivia, don't pull your weight, and act like you are a drudge or a drone, you will get accepted as that—and stay right where you are.

Look around the office. Can you spot the drudges and the drones? The worker ants? The plodders and the sloggers? Now look again and spot the high fliers, the heavyweights, the go-getters, the live wires. Can you see the difference? Can you see what you have to do? Can you see how acting the part makes you that part? Can you? Can you?

Whatever step you are preparing for, make sure that everything you do is genuine, real, and worthwhile. I once worked with a young man who was a high flier. He was preparing for his next step. He took to coming to work carrying a briefcase when none of his colleagues did—none of us needed one. Trouble is Ray's briefcase fell open one day and revealed to the entire world that all it contained was his sandwiches, a newspaper and a set of keys. It was humiliating for him, embarrassing for us, and sad for everyone. Make sure your briefcase is full of real stuff just in case this—or anything like it—happens to you.

> ONCE PEOPLE GET IN
> THE HABIT OF ASSUMING
> YOU ARE A HIGH FLIER,
> YOU BECOME ONE.

PART VIII

CULTIVATE DIPLOMACY

Smooth Rules Players move rapidly up the corporate ladder because they are diplomats. They don't start fights; they stop them. They don't sit on fences; they mend them. They spread calm around them, and others turn to them for advice and inspiration. You too will be a diplomat. You will be known for your objective appraisal of any situation, your impartial attitude, and your even-handed dealings.

RULE 80

Ask Questions in Times of Conflict

So you are at a meeting and things are getting hot under the collar. The chairman isn't handling things particularly well, and Steve and Rachael are going for each other's throats yet again. What are you going to do? Ask questions. It is easy to diffuse dangerous situations by getting the protagonists to look at some detail. You don't have to break up the fight—that's not your job. But you can be the diplomat; this gets you noticed and earns respect from your colleagues.

Turn to Steve and ask him, "Steve, why are you so convinced that your department is going to find these new invoices unworkable?" If Rachael carries on the fight, just say to her, "Hang on Rach, I really want to hear what Steve has to say." You've made it clear that you aren't taking sides but you are diffusing the situation. Hear Steve out and then turn to Rachael. "You are convinced that Steve is wrong. Tell me why?"

What you have effectively done is taken over the chair's role, become the head honcho, assumed control. This is both diplomatic and clever.

Asking questions invariably takes the heat out of potentially explosive situations. You turn to one of the combatants and ask them a simple question. Don't get bogged down in psychobabble of the "Why do you feel like that?" "Can you share your anger with us?" sort. Instead, ask them to focus on an aspect that needs explaining. They will have to break eye contact with their opponent to think about answering you. Thus, the heat dissipates, and you have proved yourself as a diplomat.

Avoid doing this if either protagonist looks like the blood has drained from his face—white face means they will hit someone, red face merely blowing hot and hard.

Avoid doing this if the chairman is handling the situation effectively—obviously, he isn't if the fight has started, but he may be making an effort and will resent your intrusion.

Avoid doing this if you are involved in the argument in any way personally.

Asking questions usually gets people to switch their attention from the main argument to a detail. They have to be pretty angry not to be polite enough to at least attempt to answer your question.

> ASKING QUESTIONS USUALLY GETS PEOPLE TO SWITCH THEIR ATTENTION FROM THE MAIN ARGUMENT TO A DETAIL.

RULE 81

Don't Take Sides

If you take sides, then you are part of the argument, the fight, the dispute, the disagreement. You have to remain totally objective and firmly in the middle. Stay on the fence whatever you do, because if you don't, then one side will blame you as well as the person she was arguing with originally. Whatever the case up for discussion you need to

- Take a long-term view
- See it from the company's point of view
- Remain impartial
- Remain calm
- Be the diplomat
- Not take sides
- Stay independent

The more detached you appear to be, the more senior you will come across. If you jump in with your boots on and take sides, you run the risk of making an enemy as well as being seen as hot headed.

The difficulty is when a friend is embroiled in a fight with another less close colleague. Your friend will invariably turn to you and try to drag you in, "Oh, for God's sake, tell her I'm right will you Rich?"

You can't afford to be dragged in. You will have to hold your hands up defensively and say, "Don't involve me. If you two can't sort this out sensibly and without arguing, I will send you both to your room." Here you have

- Made a joke of it, thus lessening the tension
- Indicated that you are senior to both of them
- Remained uninvolved
- Not taken sides

> STAY ON THE FENCE WHATEVER YOU DO, BECAUSE IF YOU DON'T, THEN ONE SIDE WILL BLAME YOU AS WELL AS THE PERSON SHE WAS ARGUING WITH ORIGINALLY.

RULE 82

Know When to Keep Your Opinions to Yourself

It's very easy to have opinions. We all have them. Trouble is knowing when to keep them to yourself and when to express them. The reason most people don't know when to shut up is that they think their opinion

- Counts for something
- Has an audience
- Is important
- Will make a difference
- Will make them seem clever/intelligent/effective
- Will win them approval/love/attention

All of these, of course, are the wrong reasons for expressing an opinion. The real reason for expressing an opinion is because you have been asked to. If you are asked, then say what you think. If you ain't been asked, then shut up.

Your opinion should almost have to be dragged from you. What you have to say is important, and you don't squander your opinions willy-nilly. You don't run off at the mouth. You don't sit there spouting opinions. You do

- Have an opinion ready for when you are asked
- Learn to express that opinion clearly and precisely and accurately
- Always make it sound as if your opinion isn't just an opinion but the actual solution that will be implemented

The way to make your opinion seem less like an opinion and more like an accepted fact is to express it as a fact. Don't say, "I think we should," instead say, "We should." Don't say, "In my opinion the ZX300 is a good machine." Instead say, "The ZX300 is a good machine."

So avoid:

- "I think"
- "I feel"
- "In my opinion"

> THE REAL REASON FOR EXPRESSING AN OPINION IS BECAUSE YOU HAVE BEEN ASKED TO.

RULE 83

Be Conciliatory

Feathers have been ruffled. You weren't involved. It was nothing to do with you. Doesn't matter. Make sure it is you who soothes those feathers.

- Make everyone a cup of coffee.
- Stroke a few egos.
- Clear the air.
- Open a window.
- Get them to shake hands (or kiss and make up).

If feathers have been ruffled by a boss telling off a junior, make sure it is the junior you comfort, cheer up, brighten up, perk up, whatever. The boss should be handled differently. The best way is the silent but disapproving action of conciliation—make him a cup of coffee but say nothing. You are indicating that you disapprove—and thus are really senior to them because you wouldn't make such a mistake—that you aren't scared of him or his anger or whatever. But maintain the silence.

If you do this well, the boss will be obliged to ask you what you thought of the way he blew up or shouted or disciplined someone. Just say, "It isn't really for me to say, is it?" Invariably, he will say, "I would value your opinion," or "No, I'd like to know," or "It's OK; say what you think." It doesn't matter what the boss says; you've got him.

Now you can be conciliatory, now you can be the diplomat, now you have turned the tables. Just say, "You handled it fine. Trish was out of order, and she needed telling." Don't, whatever you do, actually criticize the way the boss handled things.

Let him know you disapprove, but never, ever admit that in real life.

Always remember that your job isn't to make waves but to ride them. Surf your way to the top by being conciliatory. By doing this you will win friends, bring together opposing sides, and gain respect.

Being conciliatory is a bit like breaking up fights between kids. You don't want to know who started it—no, you really don't—or what it is about. You don't want the details of who pinched who or who bit who. All you want is peace restored and for them to shake hands and start over again being friends. That, at work, is all you want too. Use the same techniques you would use on small children.

> DON'T, WHATEVER YOU DO,
> ACTUALLY CRITICIZE
> THE WAY THE BOSS
> HANDLED THINGS.

Never Lose Your Temper

I don't care how annoying Pete in marketing can be or how riled you get when Sandra from R & D ridicules or how high your blood pressure rises when accounts mess it up yet again—you will not ever, under any circumstances, lose your temper. That's it. There are no exceptions. No small breaches. No thin end of any wedges. You will not lose your temper.

Not unless, of course, it is entirely staged, for effect. Then you are allowed to do it. But you have to be very careful that you have chosen the right moment, the right occasion and the right person for an audience.

But if it ain't staged then don't do it. I don't care how angry someone makes you or how annoying she can be or how justified you think you are. Loss of temper means loss of control. And the one thing a Rules Player has is control.

So how do you sit on your hands? How do you learn how to be calm and well behaved? Easy. Raise your eyes to the heavens. No, seriously. You only lose your temper if you are involved, if you care, if you are part of the problem. If you shift your focus to higher issues—the old good of the company again—it becomes easier to see whatever it is that is annoying you in a new light.

Another method is to simply leave the office or meeting or whatever. Just say, "I find this situation intolerable." And then leave. It creates quite a shock and usually does the trick.

Or try counting to 10 while you sit on your hands.

Not losing your temper doesn't mean not expressing emotion. You are entitled to say, "I find it extremely annoying when you eat all the chocolate donuts/lose the invoices/upset another major customer/park in the CEO's parking space/steal the petty cash"—whatever it is that drives you nuts.

It is OK to refuse to give in to emotional blackmail or bullying or over-assertive behavior or whining. It is not OK to bottle up stuff. Say when you feel aggrieved, immediately, so that you diffuse the situation at once. Don't let things build up a head of steam, or you may well blow. Let it out bit by bit, and it shouldn't ever come to a head.

> SAY WHEN YOU FEEL AGGRIEVED, IMMEDIATELY, SO THAT YOU DIFFUSE THE SITUATION AT ONCE.

Never Get Personal

It is their behavior that is wrong or annoying or detrimental to the department. It is never them. And it is never annoying to you, only to the good of the department. The key way to remember this is a dreadful new age thing that crept in from parenting stuff. Parents often say, "She isn't a naughty girl; she's a good girl who has done a naughty thing." Yuk. Or how about, "He is a good boy who has done a bad thing"?

This sets the scene though. It isn't the person, it is their behavior. You never ever get personal.

You can criticize

- The way they do their job
- Their time keeping, their attitude
- Their motivation
- Their communication skills
- Their long-term goals
- Their focus
- Their knowledge of office procedures
- Their appreciation of company policy
- Their inter-personal skills
- Their productivity output

But you can't ever say they are a lazy, ignorant, good for nothing, lying, thieving, bitching bastard. Oh no. Not ever. They may need retraining, relocating, reeducating, redirecting, remotivating, but never being told exactly what you really, really think of them. Getting personal will get you sacked at worst and lose you respect and friends at best.

The same goes for your boss. You may know she is useless, incompetent, corrupt, and stupid. But can you say so? No. Not even to colleagues. Remember what we said about sticking up for junior members of staff or the underdog or anyone that everyone else is having a go at? Well, your boss is the same. You always stick up for her—no matter what. You do not get personal about her, with her, or around her.

> GETTING PERSONAL WILL
> GET YOU SACKED AT
> WORST AND LOSE YOU
> RESPECT AND FRIENDS
> AT BEST.

RULE 86

Know How to Handle Other People's Anger

There will be times when you really annoy other people. In fact, being a Rules Player may get right up their noses even if they haven't a clue what it is you are doing. No one likes a smart ass and you might be seen as one if you cut loose from the herd and start looking good and looking cool. They may have a go. They may like to have a pop at you. How do you diffuse their anger?

First you have to understand that there are two types of anger:

- Justified anger
- Tactical anger.

Justified anger is exactly that—justified. You just ran over a guy's foot in your car because you weren't looking. He is quite justifiably pissed off. What do you do? You get out of the car and apologize. Say, and mean, that you are sorry. Don't deny it was your fault. Don't tell him it is nothing and he is making a bit of a fuss and you once had your entire leg ripped off and never even noticed. Don't try and explain why you weren't looking where you were going. Don't try to brush off the whole thing—"I'd have thought you'd have been pleased to have had your foot run over by a top of the range Aston Martin." And for God's sake don't laugh.

Justifiable anger needs a result. If you have done something wrong, listen to the guy—he is angry. You have made him so. Listen to what you have done wrong. And then apologize and find some way to put things right. Show the person that you sympathize—you may not be able to give him what he wants but you can still let him know that you appreciate his feelings. Don't brush his feelings aside—they are justified.

Tactical anger is, however, another thing entirely. Tactical anger is used to make you do things you don't want to. People lose their temper to intimidate you. The worst thing you can do is let them get away with it. If you do, they'll keep doing it, to you and to others. You must stop them at once. The way to do this is simply to say, "I don't like being shouted at/threatened/intimidated/bullied/whatever, and I shall leave if you don't stop/calm down/put your fists down/let go of my throat," whatever.

If they continue, then just leave. That's it. Say nothing; just walk out of the room. Do this often enough and they will get the message.

> ## FOR GOD'S SAKE DON'T LAUGH.

RULE 87

Stand Your Ground

No one is allowed to bully you, threaten you, shout at you, hit you, intimidate you, frighten you, tease you, victimize you, or torment you in any way. You are an employee. If you aren't doing your job properly, you should be taken to one side and have your mistakes pointed out calmly and rationally. Anything else is abuse.

You are allowed to refuse abuse. You are allowed, calmly and rationally, to tell someone to stop at once or you are entitled to use the full weight of the law to get someone to stop. You have to know when to stand your ground.

Obviously, if someone is mildly teasing—the same as everyone else gets—then you can't walk out and claim unfair dismissal. If your boss snaps at you occasionally—the same as they do to all employees—you can't demand the Court of Human Rights has them strung up, even if they are out of order. If a colleague says she'll give you a slap if you take her hole puncher again, you can't really expect the Supreme Court to take up your case. We are talking real abuse here, not the sort of rough and tumble you'd expect in the tumult of a busy working life.

Standing your ground is about having standards, drawing a line in the sand, and saying, "I will put up with this, but not this," or "I will allow them to do this to me, but not this."

One approach is to ask the person open questions. This avoids trying to be underhand and playing the same game she is, and if you do it in front of other people, it can put the person on the spot and make her feel very uncomfortable and she'll learn to think twice about putting you in that situation again. So, at a meeting you can ask politely, "Why did you not tell me about this at last week's meeting? It would clearly have been useful information for me to have." Then keep quiet so the onus is on her to justify herself. Or say, "I feel put down when you make rude remarks. Why do you do it?" That should put a stop to their nasty ways.

Standing your ground is about having standards, drawing a line in the sand, and saying, "I will put up with this, but not this."

Standing your ground is about being assertive. Being assertive is about stating your bottom line: "I don't appreciate being locked in dark cupboards and I shall have to report this incident to my union representative/boss/the police/the health and safety committee/my mother."

If bullied, stick to the stuck record—"I don't appreciate being treated like this. I don't appreciate being treated like this. I don't appreciate being treated like this." Don't lose your temper, or the bully may feel they have "won." Walk away.

> STANDING YOUR GROUND
> IS ABOUT BEING
> ASSERTIVE.

RULE 88

Be Objective About the Situation

If you are feeling abused and tormented at work, you have various choices:

- Walk
- Report it
- Flair up and be angry
- Say nothing
- Handle it assertively

How you choose to handle difficult situations is entirely up to you. However, before you react, think of the long-term plan. How will a claim for unfair dismissal or constructive dismissal look on your resume over a career history? I'm not saying you should put up with abuse of any sort just to get on. No, I am not saying that at all. I am saying be objective about the situation.

I was once ridiculed by a particular boss—and badly ridiculed. This man had got it into his head that I was his pet football to be kicked around as and when he felt like it—and that was, curiously, often after boozy lunches. I was quite junior and had few choices—walk away from the job or go over his head and report him. But his boss was also his best friend. If I reported him, I would have been out on my ear pretty quick. I needed the job and didn't want to walk away. I had to be quite devious, but I basically got him to treat me badly—ridiculing, abusive language, that sort of thing—when one of our major customers was listening.

My boss didn't know this, and the customer was furious. He sorted my boss out in no uncertain terms. Said he ought to be ashamed of himself treating a junior like that. Tore him off a good strip indeed and then told me to tell him if this ever happened again—and that if it did he would take his business elsewhere. His business was about 70 percent of our entire turnover.

My boss had to apologize to me in front of the customer. And I wasn't treated badly again. I felt I was objective. I then waited, and sure enough he acted up again with someone else and was eventually sacked. I waved him goodbye with a cheery grin and a wink.

> BEFORE YOU REACT,
> THINK OF THE
> LONG-TERM PLAN.

PART IX

KNOW THE SYSTEM—AND MILK IT

If you are going to move on up, you had better know the ropes. These Rules teach you how to understand the system—and how to milk it for all you're worth. They will have you out-managing the management because you'll know the system better than they do.

Know All the Unspoken Rules of Office Life

There are a whole heap of unwritten Rules in any workplace. These might be as simple as who is "allowed" to use which elevator/break room/restroom/corridor/outside smoking area, or as complex as who holds the keys to the petty cash/photo-copier/ stationery cupboard/vacation schedule. I have often known the strangest people doing duties that no one has ever given them. I once worked in an office where a Swiss transla-tor was in charge of the vacation schedule. Why, for heaven's sake?

You had to get your vacation approved by her, logged by her, and permitted by her. But why her? Whenever I asked, I was told it was historical that the translators did the vacations. It was bizarre, stupid, really off the wall. My supervisor should have done them, but I guess he was quite pleased that the translators had taken this "burden" off his shoulders. Weird.

If you have been in your job for a while, you should have learned all these rules by now. If new, then these things are waiting to be found out. OK, so you know these rules; what use are they to you? Easy. It's a bit like the unions used to be—working to an obscure rule book that the management never really understood or knew. You will be able to outmaneuvre anyone by knowing these unwritten Rules.

I went to work in an office where the most junior had to take the most senior boss his coffee in the mornings and the unwritten rule was that this junior would wait while he drank the coffee. The junior didn't "have" to, it was just expected of him. I was that junior. For about five minutes every day I had the ultimate boss's undivided attention. I had the ear of the highest. I had access to God. I milked it, as you might have guessed.

I got my department head moved to another department. He was unpopular and I merely mentioned to the big boss that the department head had certain skills that he hadn't revealed, but that would come in very useful in the new department. He was moved.

> YOU WILL BE ABLE TO OUTMANEUVRE ANYONE BY KNOWING THESE UNWRITTEN RULES.

RULE 90

Know What to Call Everyone

Yes, you should know what to call everyone, but that doesn't mean you are going to call them that. I dare say Mr. Cutler has long since forgotten me. I was his assistant many years ago. When he changed companies he phoned me and asked me to join the new firm with him—more money, etc.—so I said yes.

On my first day working with him at the new company, he said to me, "Call me Mr. Cutler." No way, Peter. I had called him Peter at the old place and was going to carry on calling him that. But not quite yet. There were several assistants, and they needed to get to know this new boss, this Mr. Cutler. That's what they called him, because that's what he wanted. I waited until the moment was right and we were all gathered together. Then I addressed him as Peter.

He couldn't pull me up short in front of my peers and they thought, quite rightly, that I had secret access to him that they didn't. For me the Mr. Cutler nonsense was never mentioned again and I was the "senior" assistant because I called him Peter. What's in a name? A whole lot.

You need to know that Mrs. Robertson in accounts is always addressed as Mrs. Robertson and never as Mary, although you know that is her name and you are senior to her. Why not call her Mary? Because she doesn't like it and she handles the paychecks. They have been known to go astray, be very late, be made out for much less than the anticipated amount—and all to people who inadvertently called her Mary.

In one job, I worked with an administrative manager who was known, for curious reasons, as Buckethead. It's a long story, and you really don't want to know. (No, believe me, you really don't.) He was addressed to his face as Buckethead by all the senior staff—including me as finance manager. He was Buckethead to the board. He was Buckethead to most of the secretarial staff. But anyone else and he was Mr. Taylor, never Buckethead. I have seen him savage a young junior who made the mistake and called him Buckethead. Now why this strange division between who could and who could not call him that name? I have no idea but I did have a very strange relationship with him. Technically, he was my senior, albeit if only slightly. But I was power hungry in those days, and I wanted to control everything. I never ever called him Buckethead. I didn't like him. To me he was always Mr. Taylor. Why? Because it separated us and made me different from the other senior managers. I stood alone and Buckethead could never get close to me, never be a "friend." I played the aloof game and was eventually offered the general managership of the company, which would have made him my junior. Success? Yes, but it felt a hollow victory—I wasn't playing the Rules as effectively then as now—and I left for new challenges, new horizons.

> ## "CALL ME MR. CUTLER."
> ## NO WAY, PETER.

Know When to Stay Late and When to Go Early

There is an unwritten rule that if you want to move up you have to stay late because everyone else stays late. Clones stay late. Drones stay late. Worker ants stay late. Rules Players go home when they want to—and that is invariably earlier than anyone else.

It's the same with arriving in the office in the morning. Who says you have to arrive early? No one. It is one of those unwritten rules we need to know, so we can adapt it to our own ends.

The object of the exercise is to be *thought* to be working as hard as everyone else. The game is to get away with being thought of as a conformist, a drone, when in fact you don't have to because you are so much better than that. You get your work done in record time so you don't have to stay late.

If you ever watch motivational speakers, they always put their hand up when they ask you—and the rest of the audience—a question. This sets the lead, and you automatically put your hand up because there is already one hand up in the room. Silly, isn't it? But it only takes one of you to leave at a reasonable time for everyone else to follow suit. Staying because you think everyone else is staying is called "presenteeism" and is a curse of modern office life. We all think that everyone else is watching us, as we are watching them, to see who will be the first to break, to leave, to incur the boss's wrath.

It is, however, a myth. The first to leave isn't going to be missing anything. That person will be liberating the rest of us. Leave now and set us free, please.

The fear of missing something is very real. But if we are leading exciting and interesting lives, we know that we are the center of the universe and that the others who stay behind are the ones who are in reality missing out, missing something, missing in action.

People think that leaving early—or at the right time actually, the time we are contracted to leave—will draw undue attention to us, make us seem to be shirkers. But if we leave confidently and honestly, this doesn't happen. We only get viewed badly for leaving before others if we slink out, leave by the back door, creep away into the night with our tail between our legs. So wave boldly and tell them, "Last one to leave turns out the lights." Whether it is fair to point out that if they were any good at their jobs they too, like you, would have finished their work on time is debatable. You are allowed to think it though.

> ## THE FEAR OF MISSING SOMETHING IS VERY REAL.

RULE 92

Know the Theft or Perks Rule

So what can you take home? Pens? Paperclips? Staplers? When is it a perk and when is it theft? You should know this, as it can come in useful if you want to have a hold over someone—the someone who thinks nothing of taking home everything that ain't actually screwed down. Watch what they take, and make a mental note of it. This might come in useful. You, of course, will take nothing.

I have known an entire department cleared out because a new manager suddenly got it into his head that they were all committing grand larceny because they took home copies of all the software used by the computers. At home they all had the latest Windows, Word, and Outlook Express but a lot of good it did them when they had to sign on.

Was it theft? It doesn't matter. It got them the sack. If one of them had been known not to do this, they would have survived. If one of them had known the new manager's views on perks, they might have survived.

Before you start filling your pockets, make sure it is worth it. Are those pens really that attractive? Will you be able to sell enough cheap pens to feed your family for however long it takes you to find a new job?

We've looked at the unwritten rules of office life. One of these might be that you do take home perks. And if you choose not to, make sure you don't get labeled as a teacher's pet or goody-goody or anything else that could get you ostracised. Be part of the herd even if you steal nothing. Let your boss know you don't, but make the staff think you are the same as they are.

And watch out for the free phone calls and the Internet connection. These might not qualify as take home perks, but it is still theft to make free phone calls when you aren't allowed to. There is a good chance they get monitored, so don't do it.

Fiddling expenses can be part of the office culture. If you don't do it, it can blow the whistle on the others who do. So what do you do? You have to be honest and above board, but you can't rat on your colleagues. Ask the audience? Phone a friend? Doing it might seem the lesser of two evils, but you are a Rules Player now and can't condone such activity. Better to say in advance to your colleagues that they can do what they like or want, but you won't be a party to such irregularities. Warn them beforehand, and then if they still insist on doing it, you haven't dropped them in it.

> BEFORE YOU START
> FILLING YOUR POCKETS,
> MAKE SURE IT IS
> WORTH IT.

RULE 93

Identify the People Who Count

I once made a bad mistake—well, I've probably made lots, but this one is relevant and sticks in my mind. I worked for a company and we had a maintenance man. At the end of each day, we wrote in the maintenance book anything that needed doing, such as changing light bulbs, and plunging toilets, and Harry would do it. Mending broken chairs, that sort of thing. We had two offices, and I used to get quite cross that Harry seemed to spend more time down at the other branch than at our place. Harry was never anywhere to be found.

My notes in the maintenance book grew terse and sharper, but it didn't seem to do any good. I would have rollicked Harry in person if ever I'd have been able to find him. He came in after we had gone home and did the maintenance work in the evenings. The other office was getting all their repairs done, and we were getting nothing done. It was intolerable, and I resolved one evening to wait for Harry.

Harry didn't show, so I went over to the other office. There was Harry having coffee with the big boss, my regional director. I steamed in—"What the devil do you think you're doing? I need you over at the other place doing maintenance, not sitting here drinking coffee!" Bad mistake. Several bad mistakes:

- You don't bawl someone out for drinking coffee when they were on an official " coffee-break."
- You don't bawl someone out for drinking coffee when they have been invited to do so by the regional director.
- You don't bawl someone out in front of your regional director without first checking all the salient facts with him.

- You do things properly—go through the appropriate channels and don't hide in wait for an errant worker.
- You always *identify the people who count*—in this case, Harry.

Why did Harry count? Because he was my regional director's father-in-law. He had juice and power and influence that I could only dream of. He was working at the other office because he had been told to by his son-in-law. As I said, bad mistake.

I've worked for companies where it was the cashier, the CEO's driver, the accountant, and the lunch room chef who had the juice. Invariably, it took some time to identify these people. They all held some trump card that gave them access to a senior boss, or had some hold over them such as being a relative. Find them, know them.

> WHY DID HARRY COUNT?
> BECAUSE HE WAS MY
> REGIONAL DIRECTOR'S
> FATHER-IN-LAW.

Be on the Right Side of the People Who Count

So how do you think I got along with Harry after my out-burst? Our relationship was bad beforehand. Now it positively stank. Do you think I could get a light bulb changed? No way, not now, not ever. Identifying the people who count and being on the right side of them go hand in hand, obviously.

I once worked with an auditor who was a complete you-know-what. Everything had to be done by the book. Every i dotted and t crossed. This man would have made Attila the Hun look like a charity worker. But this was a man who counted. Not only was he the auditor, he seemed to have juice far beyond his role as an accountant. This was a man the senior manage-ment bowed to, listened to, sought advice from, dared not cross, and were in fear of, and they generally treated him like royalty.

I never quite got to the bottom of why he wielded so much influence, but I had to work with it. And once I had identified him I had to get on the right side of him. I hadn't been up to then. As finance manager, my department came under his scrutiny constantly and closely.

I had upset Harry at every step along the way. We didn't see eye to eye. He was an accountant and I was a finance manager—there is quite a difference. My brief was to install security systems, improve cash flow, cut costs, and tighten all fiscal procedures. His was to audit every penny.

I took my kids to a garage sale one Saturday morning. It was autumn and I felt cold, so I bought a college scarf at the sale. You know the sort, stripy, dark, traditional. On Monday I wore it into work. I bumped into the auditor in the corridor. "Ah," he said "I didn't know you went to Manchester University. Well done." And he walked off.

I hadn't a clue what he was talking about until it dawned on me that the scarf was a Manchester University scarf. This was the university the auditor had gone to (no, I hadn't gone there, or to any university) and from then on he accepted me as one of his own, a chum, an old college pal. I could do no wrong.

This was an accident. Since then I have engineered such incidents to get on the right side of the people who count, the ones who have influence who shouldn't. These are the ones who have juice incommensurate with their position or job.

There is a group of people you should watch out for—they often have unaccountable juice—which includes drivers, auditors, PR people, human resource people, assistants, people who have been with the company for a very long time, outside consultants, free agents, cashiers, ex-employees, and of course, maintenance people!

> THESE ARE THE ONES
> WHO HAVE JUICE
> INCOMMENSURATE WITH
> THEIR POSITION OR JOB.

RULE 95

Be Well Up on New Management Techniques

You cannot afford ever to stand still, to rest on your laurels, to sit back and take it easy. All the time you are doing any of these things, there will be someone stealing up on you.

You have to move with the times, and that means keeping up with the latest management techniques, the newest buzzwords, whatever is executive flavor of the month. To stay top of the tree, you have to know what jargon is being talked. It's no good referring to it as personnel when everyone else is talking about human resources. You'll look a chump if you are still stuck in logistics when the board are now concentrating on client-focused core business or whatever.

I'm not suggesting you have to use these new techniques, but you had better know them to stay ahead of the pack—you may be asked. You can always have fun playing buzzword bingo at meetings—award yourself a point for every new ridiculous buzzword you hear and when you have 10 points leap to your feet and shout, "Bingo!" It keeps you awake.

And you'll certainly hear a lot of wonderfully useless expressions—for instance, what exactly does Blue Sky mean? As in, "We shall have to Blue Sky this product." It might mean, "Anything goes, be creative, and set no boundaries." It might also mean, "We're a bunch of jargonists who want to sound cool and with it but who actually sound rather silly."

If you use buzzwords, try not to sound silly. You should, of course, know what they all mean.

You should also know what all the latest management disciplines are and how they might affect you. Try not to sound out of date when you talk of management techniques. For instance, it was called logistics in my day, but now it is supply chain management—and by the time you are reading this it will be something else, I expect.

You should know what the advantages and disadvantages of any of these buzzwords are just in case they crop up and you want to look good. There ought to be a sort of bluffer's guide to management speak, but I don't think there is. You will have to incorporate it into your game plan and see the big picture because at the end of the day there will be a new ball park, and the best practice of your core business will be a sort of knock-on effect that will play you out of the loop if you don't take your knowledge off-line and start thinking outside the box. That kind of thinking might just get you in with the movers and shakers without having to move your goal posts or go the extra mile while playing hardball and being a show stopper. So push the envelope, and the bottom line is total quality.

> TRY NOT TO SOUND OUT OF DATE WHEN YOU TALK OF MANAGEMENT TECHNIQUES.

RULE 96

Know the Undercurrents and Hidden Agendas

When your boss says he wants to improve customer relations and you should all go on a course to learn how to smile, don't be fooled. It's nothing to do with smiling at customers. Your boss is coming up for appraisal time and needs to look good, needs to appear as if there is some drive, initiative, and motivation.

So you'll all troop off and do the course and try to take it all in and practice your smile. What for? Your boss couldn't give two monkeys whether you smile at the customers or not. All he wants is to shine at his appraisal.

This sort of thing goes on a lot more at work than most people like to think. Once, I volunteered to attend college every Monday to do a course in payroll and double entry bookkeeping. My boss thought I was keen, self-motivated, and very enthusiastic. Nonsense. I wanted to get out of the office every Monday because that was the day we had to do all the filing and I hated it. Going to college seemed a good cop-out.

Question the motives of everyone and everything. This doesn't mean you have to become paranoid. No one is out to get you. All you need to do is watch out for the hidden agenda. It might not affect you in any way, but it will be fun to spot what is really going on.

I once worked for a boss who always liked to be the last to leave. I thought him conscientious and industrious. It was only when he had been arrested for fraud that I realized that staying after everyone else had gone was his opportunity to fiddle the books. And there was little old me admiring his keen spirit.

Always ask:

- Why is this happening?
- Is there anything I am missing?
- Who benefits from this?
- How are they benefiting?
- What else could be going on?
- Can I benefit from this?
- How?

As I said, don't get paranoid; get the facts.

YOUR BOSS IS COMING UP FOR APPRAISAL TIME AND NEEDS TO LOOK GOOD.

Know the Favorites and Cultivate Them

Every boss has a favorite. I know they/we shouldn't, but it is human nature. It goes on because we/they are all human, and even parents have favorites although they would never admit it.

There are two parts to this rule:

- If favoritism is going on—and it will be—make sure you are your boss's favorite
- Make sure you know all the favorites in other departments.

If you have got a boss who is going to have favorites, you can buck the system or try being the favorite. If you do become a favorite, don't for heaven's sake flaunt it among your colleagues. Be self-effacing and deny it, be humble and don't acknowledge it, be modest and pretend it ain't going on.

To get to be a favorite has to depend on skill, presence, charisma, talent, expertise, experience, likeability, charm, personal affability. It must never depend on brownnosing, fawning, obsequiousness, or flattery. You have to earn being a favorite, not worm your way in. If you do, you will be hated by your colleagues. If you genuinely deserve it because you are dependable or reliable or efficient or honest, then your colleagues will just about put up with it.

Spotting the favorites in other departments should be fairly easy. They will be treated pretty much as you are. They will

- Get the first pick on the vacation schedule
- Be trusted, a confidante

- Be invited to meetings
- Get the prestigious jobs and the perks
- Be chatted to by the boss rather than being barked at

Once spotted, make a friend of them. This way you will know what is going on, be in with the in-crowd, have the ear of the boss of other departments, and have joined an elite. If, on the other hand, you really disapprove of favoritism, do none of this.

> YOU HAVE TO EARN BEING
> A FAVORITE, NOT WORM
> YOUR WAY IN.

RULE 98

Know the Mission Statement— and Understand It

In the good old days, a company's mission statement was probably: "Make as much money as possible and keep the shareholders off our back." Not any more it ain't. A mission statement is now much more complex. If you want to make a success of your employment, you have to know and understand the mission statement—and then milk it for all you are worth. Quoting the mission statement earns you brownie points if you make sure it looks as if you are really on the side of the company. If your boss doesn't support the mission statement or considers such things as rubbish and not worth bothering with, then keep quiet about mission statements.

To understand the mission statement is usually quite easy— Walt Disney's "To make people happy," Wal-Mart's "To give ordinary folk the chance to buy the same thing as rich people"—but to really understand it, you have to read all the small print. For instance, Disney's is quite simple but there is a whole lot more because they also have a "value statement" that covers:

- No cynicism
- Creativity, dreams and imagination
- Nurturing and promulgation of "wholesome American values"
- Fanatical attention to consistency and detail
- Preservation and control of the Disney "magic"

If you can't find something here—assuming you work for Disney—to milk, you aren't worthy of calling yourself a Rules Player. Imagine what fun you could have with some of these. Imagine what power you would wield at meetings just quoting some of this. Someone suggests an idea you don't like, you could just say it isn't wholesomely American. Brilliant. It's like being part of the Spanish Inquisition—our chief weapons are ... Among our many weapons are such diverse ...

Some historical mission statements were very grand and could have safely been milked for all they were worth:

- Ford (early 1900s)—Ford will democratize the automobile.
- Sony (early 1950s)—To become the company most known for changing the worldwide poor-quality image of Japanese products.
- Boeing (1950)—To become the dominant player in commercial aircraft and bring the world into the jet age.
- Wal-Mart (1990)—To become a $125 billion company by the year 2000.

QUOTING THE MISSION
STATEMENT EARNS YOU
BROWNIE POINTS IF YOU
MAKE SURE IT LOOKS AS IF
YOU ARE REALLY ON THE
SIDE OF THE COMPANY.

PART X

HANDLE THE OPPOSITION

If there's a promotion going and five possible candidates, how do you identify them? And then how do you make yourself the obvious choice? Here's how you identify the competition—your competition. And then make yourself the favorite without being ruthless or underhand. In fact, if you practice these Rules really well, you will get them to recommend you, and want you to be promoted ahead of them.

Identify the Opposition

So, there is a chance for promotion. You want it. You want that next step up. This promotion fits in with your long-term plan. This is the ideal time and opportunity for you to make that step. Trouble is you aren't alone in the running. There are other people to take into account—and eliminate, of course. Obviously, for any appointment there are two categories of candidates:

- The internal candidate
- The external candidate

The internal ones are your immediate colleagues, staff from other departments, staff from other branches, staff from other disciplines. If it's your immediate colleagues, chances are you know full well who is interested and who isn't. Staff from other departments should be identified by checking your sources—you should have the ear of every favorite in every department (*see Rule 97*). Staff from other branches present a bit of a challenge, but you should use your contacts for such information (*Rule 52*). Candidates from other disciplines within the same organization are the real test. Often you won't know about them until they suddenly appear at the interview stage. When I worked for American Express way back in the early 1970s, I was in line for a promotion to department supervisor. I had eliminated all the potential competition from among my own colleagues, checked out the opposition from other departments and branches—there wasn't any—and felt secure and relaxed when, hey presto, a new candidate appeared from a completely separate but parallel discipline. I was accounts and this person was from security. Security, I ask you; what did this person know about accounts supervision? The senior management obviously thought he knew a great deal because he got the job. I hadn't had the chance to disable him. I was taken unawares. Never again.

Candidates from outside the company are very tricky. You have no idea who will apply. But you can

- See the advert before it goes to press and have a pretty good idea of what is being asked for
- Use contacts to find out who is on the shortlist from outside
- Again use contacts to find out who is being called for interview and what sort of competition you are up against

Remember that knowledge is power. You may not like what you find out, but at least you will know.

> ## USE CONTACTS TO FIND OUT WHO IS BEING CALLED FOR INTERVIEW AND WHAT SORT OF COMPETITION YOU ARE UP AGAINST.

RULE 100

Study Them Closely

If you are going for a promotion and there is competition, you need to read, understand, and completely grasp what is being asked for. You need to tailor your resume, application document, and interview technique so that you fully fit the picture of the ideal candidate. And you have to study what the competition is doing. Suppose the job is for a supervisory departmental head of the computer sales division. You know that you have

- Experience of sales
- Experience of computers
- But little experience of supervising other staff

Now check out the opposition. Suppose there are two other candidates:

- Tony has a good working knowledge of the products and good supervisory experience but knows nothing about sales.
- Sandra is good on the sales side and has excellent supervisory experience but doesn't understand the product at all.

Who is the ideal candidate? It depends entirely on what the management is looking for—or what they think they are looking for. The job obviously needs three parts—sales, product knowledge and supervisory duties. You have two out of three—as do the other two candidates. But which one is the most important to the management? You need to check this out carefully:

- Read the job description
- Liaise with whoever is doing the job now
- Research what the management is thinking

If the focus is on one of the two areas you are strong in, then you have already eliminated one of the candidates. Now it's a two-horse race. If, however, the third option is the focus—supervision—the one area you are weak in, then you will have to swing the focus more toward your own skills and experience. At interview you will have to find good reasons why your lack of experience doesn't discount you—talk up the product and how essential it is to have a good knowledge of it and its potential, talk up the importance of sales and how the department lives or dies by its sales record.

Obviously, this is just an example; the real world is much more complicated.

WHO IS THE
IDEAL CANDIDATE?
IT DEPENDS ENTIRELY ON
WHAT THE MANAGEMENT
IS LOOKING FOR.

Don't Back-Stab

The one thing you won't do in your race to the top is back-stab. You will not take out the opposition by unlawful means. It is OK to talk up your own talents and skills and to cleverly influence what management is looking for by highlighting your own expertise and the implied failings of your competition. You can imply, suggest, and insinuate. What you cannot do is state openly and honestly why you think they are useless. You make out that they are not up to the promotion by getting the management to focus on how good you are, not by pointing out how bad they are.

The things you do not do are

- Bad-mouth the opposition
- Back-stab the competition
- Speak ill of anyone
- Tell lies about the other contestants (*see Rule 48*)
- Reveal secret information about the competition that you have found out that could affect their chances
- Steal information
- Peek, pry, or spy

These are what you must not do. But what can you do then? Well, you can

- Use any contacts you have to find out the calibre of the competition
- Enhance your own attributes creatively based on what the management is looking for

- Talk up your own good points, highlighting special skills and expertise you have that they are lacking—you don't say they haven't got what it takes; you make sure the management knows that you do
- Sell management something they may not have even known they wanted, which the opposition hasn't got

> THE ONE THING YOU
> WON'T DO IN YOUR RACE
> TO THE TOP IS BACK-STAB.

Know the Psychology of Promotion

Suppose a vacancy has arisen internally. You quite fancy the job, it fits in with your game plan, and you could do with the extra money. You have the expertise, the experience, and the qualifications. You think you will apply for the post. All well and good. But what is being decided here? And what are the criteria being used?

You think job X is vacant; therefore, person Y will fill the post just so long as she has the right attributes. But what are the right attributes? Oh, I know you'll say

- Experience
- Qualifications
- Expertise

Just like you've got, and that's why you are a perfect candidate. Not quite true, I'm afraid. There is usually a whole lot more going on than you know. For instance, the post may be being advertised because

- Head office says it has to be but your management has no intention of filling it.
- Your manager has already unofficially filled it—it's been offered to someone already in secret.
- The job is being downsized; it will go to someone who will be made redundant in six months' time,
- The whole exercise is a waste of time. The person already doing the job has resigned but he is going to withdraw that at the last minute—he's just holding out for more money at the moment.

- It's an exercise in getting rid of someone; they'll offer it to someone completely unsuitable so they have grounds to sack the person, which they can't do in their current position
- The job is being created so the manager can give it to their favorite/lover/friend/relative/blackmailer.

I don't want to make you paranoid, but there are a million and one reasons why you may not get the job despite being, on paper, the best person for it. There may also be a million reasons why you shouldn't apply. You have to know all this. Study the psychology of whatever is being offered. It may not be quite what it seems.

STUDY THE PSYCHOLOGY OF WHATEVER IS BEING OFFERED. IT MAY NOT BE QUITE WHAT IT SEEMS.

Don't Give Too Much Away

It is probably advisable not to tell anyone that you

- Intend on applying for a new position within the company
- Intend on applying for a new job outside of the company
- Are thinking of leaving anyway
- Are thinking of asking for a pay rise
- Are thinking of changing your working schedules
- Are a Rules Player

Don't blab to anyone of anything you are doing. It might be seen as bragging—a Rules Player never brags about anything, we are quiet humility itself—or it might give rise to gossip, and we know the Rule about that, don't we? And the truth is that even if you only tell one person things leak out. She tells her closest friend and he tells his. And so on it goes until you are being hauled before the boss and interrogated as to why you are leaving next Monday when all you had done was say you were thinking about it to Susan in the break room. If you do reveal stuff about yourself, you are open to

- Rumor, gossip, and an opportunity for others to possibly use it against you
- Giving the opposition an unfair advantage
- Giving the management information they shouldn't be privy to at this stage

Don't even allow yourself the privilege of thinking out loud. Keep your own counsel, and you won't go far wrong. What you intend doing is entirely up to you. If you need information and anyone asks you why you need it, invent something entirely bogus. No, this is not lying; it is throwing someone off the scent. Don't lie, but you can be circumspect, devious, inventive, creative, eccentric, and you are allowed to set up a decoy.

If someone asks you directly if you are thinking about applying for a particular position, you can always brush it off, "Oh, always thinking about applying." Does this mean yes or no? Remember: don't lie and say, "No," when it is plainly untrue and will be seen to be such when you do apply.

> KEEP YOUR OWN COUNSEL,
> AND YOU WON'T GO
> FAR WRONG.

Keep Your Ear to the Ground

If you don't know what is going on, how can you make informed decisions or coordinate your career plan? It might be as simple as someone applying for a position you had in mind. If that person is more experienced, better qualified, and has more expertise and skill in that area, then you might be sensible holding back. If you don't you will probably fail—and a Rules Player is always successful.

Now you don't want gossip; you want hard facts. You want to know what is going on without having to listen to gossip and idle chit-chat. Therefore, it makes sense to

- Use your contacts for information from other departments
- Pay attention at meetings—it is often surprising how much information you can pick up by reading between the lines
- Watch and listen for the "hidden agendas"—what people are saying might mask what is really going on
- Cultivate the office favorite/s and you'll find that they invariably know stuff mere mortals aren't privy to—you'll just have to get them to spill the beans
- Keep abreast of things like the trade press as you may pick up bits of information that have been "leaked" to the press before the rank and file have been told—that new merger, the takeover, the acquisition of a rival company, all these can be useful snippets of information that can put you one step ahead of colleagues and competitors

RULE 104

A lot of people don't get anywhere with their job because they spend far too much time doing their job. You need to get your head up from time to time and look around you. You might find the herd has moved on while you were busy feeding and now you are alone and forgotten.

> YOU NEED TO GET YOUR HEAD UP FROM TIME TO TIME AND LOOK AROUND YOU.

RULE 105

Make the Opposition Seem Irreplaceable

We have looked at why you can't indulge in any back-stabbing—*Rule 101: Don't Back-Stab*—and you know you can't say anything bad about anyone, but all the same, one of the competition is getting in a bit too close with the boss and it looks like that promotion might just go their way. What do you do? You make them seem irreplaceable, of course. But you do it by pointing out all the important but mundane jobs they do. You point out their strengths to your boss in the boring, humdrum areas. "God, I don't know what we'd do without Rachael to do the filing. She must be a Virgo—she's so good at that sort of stuff." But you are only going to point out things that your rival is genuinely good at. We are not going to lie—*Rule 48: Never Lie*—but merely praise the competition for a particular skill. And a skill that they can best exercise right where they are.

Your boss is your customer—you sell your services to them. Your colleagues are the competition. If you were selling cars and someone asked if the next garage sold better cars, what would you say? You wouldn't say, "Yes, they sell much better cars than us—and cheaper; in fact you ought to go straight there and buy one of theirs right now." But you also wouldn't say anything bad—"Their cars are all stolen"—though you might well say, "Their cars are fine but they appeal to a different customer; they sell more family saloons than we do." You haven't lied. You have indirectly flattered your customer—the implication being, "You obviously need a much more up-market executive car than those shoddy little boxes they sell next door"—but you haven't said anything bad.

You can also get your rival colleague to ask questions of themselves about the new position: "If you did get Richard's job, how do you think you'd cope with all those meetings? I remember your telling me you hated meetings." Hopefully she'll think about all those dreary interminable, intimidating meetings and may well back off. You, on the other hand, find them stimulating, exciting, and very productive—and you haven't said anything bad, merely asked a simple question. You'll get them to want to stay right where they are—they'll make themselves irreplaceable.

> **YOUR BOSS IS YOUR CUSTOMER. YOUR COLLEAGUES ARE THE COMPETITION.**

Don't Damn the Opposition with Faint Praise

The last Rule may have seemed as if we were approaching something underhand or devious or ruthless. It isn't. Everything has to be meant, genuine, and honest. Don't praise them. Not unless you really mean it. It is so easy to undermine someone by using praise when you are actually being rather horrid and stitching them up. You may think this a clever approach. It isn't. You will be seen through immediately and come across as shallow, vindictive, and really rather ruthless. *Remember: If you can't say anything nice—shut up?* Well, you may think that you can get away with saying nasty things, disguised as nice things, but you can't. This is the sort of thing that is forbidden:

- "Oh, I know Bill is brilliantly wacky. He is such an independent thinker. He really does operate outside of the box; he's so original and off the wall."

What you're really saying: he's a lone wolf who is slightly mad and shouldn't be trusted supervising a chimps' coffe break let alone an entire department:

- "Bill is such a determined worker. He doesn't care how much it costs; he goes for the last detail of a job. Superb resolution. He likes to see things through to the very end, no matter what. I admire his ability to just see not just the dollar signs on a project but the application."

What you're really saying: he should never be trusted with his own money, let alone someone else's:

- "Bill really is one of the guys. He really knows how to let his hair down and have fun. I admire his ability to hold his liquor. If there's a wacky stunt going on, Bill is always in the thick of it; he is such a free spirit and so youth orientated."

What you're really saying: he's a drunk, a bit wild, not to be trusted looking after staff,s and he has the mental age of a teenager:

- "We can't keep Bill in the office. He's such a live wire. I don't think our little cage is big enough for someone with that much energy. I envy him. I sit here doing the paperwork while he's off, out there talking to customers and liaising and being brilliant at sales."

What you're really saying: Bill is crap at paperwork. Don't get into this trap. Your seniors will see through it, and if they are decent people they aren't going to like it.

> WELL, YOU MAY THINK
> THAT YOU CAN GET AWAY
> WITH SAYING NASTY
> THINGS, DISGUISED
> AS NICE THINGS, BUT
> YOU CAN'T.

Capitalize on the Career-Enhancing Moments

Every now and then there is a break from the routine, the humdrum, the everyday. These moments of intense activity or public limelight are your moments to enhance your career. They can be

- The initial selection interview
- Your first day
- Running a presentation
- Running an exhibition
- Chairing an important meeting
- Being put in charge of staff training
- Handling a crisis
- Negotiating with the unions
- Attending a health and safety committee meeting
- Being a first aider
- Organizing the staff function
- Being responsible for the visit of a dignitary, celebrity, or royalty
- Editing the newsletter
- Dealing with the media
- Supervising the office relocation

A lot of people, when first presented with such an option, will be filled with dismay and horror. "Oh, no," they cry, "Not running the exhibition stand at the NEC this year. Why me? Oh Lord, why me?"

You, on the other hand, know this rule—this is a career-enhancing moment and you had better take the opportunity to shine. There are no bad jobs, only bad attitudes to jobs.

Always look for ways of making such jobs better, more interesting, slicker, and quicker, and realize that they are providing you with the means to shine.

> THERE ARE NO BAD JOBS,
> ONLY BAD ATTITUDES
> TO JOBS.

Cultivate the Friendship and Approval of Your Colleagues

If you follow all the rules outlined in this book, you will be a thoroughly nice person, likeable, confident, agreeable, and assured. You will be grown up but still a lot of fun to be around. You need the support of your fellow coworkers to move up, and you need their friendship and approval. If you don't have these things, you open yourself up to the possibility of being set up, pulled down, dumped upon, or seen off. But how do you cultivate their friendship and approval when you are doing everything to get promoted above them, to be their boss?

What you have to do is be one of the girls/guys while retaining a modicum of detachment. You have to run with the sheep and hunt with the wolves. You have to be "one of them" and one of the bosses.

You'll need to socialize with the staff without losing control, getting drunk, sleeping with any of them, or getting involved. Laugh at their jokes, but don't go on vacation with them. Listen to their troubles, but don't tell them they are trivial or inconsequential. Support them and nurture them when they are under pressure, but remain calm at all times yourself. You have to become their mother hen at the same time as their friend and fellow conspirator. You have to listen to their complaints and moans about management and the boss without revealing who you really are—their eventual new boss.

You have to help them with their work so they get to rely on you. You have to be the diplomat, the conciliator, the referee, the pal, and the priest. You have to get them to love you because you are so nice, so friendly yourself.

You have to be their tower of strength and their prop and their chum. You have to make them feel special, feel that without you their lives are gray and dull and boring. You have to be the life and soul of the party and the party organizer and the one who clears up afterward.

All this is possible—not easy but possible. If you get on the right side of your colleagues to such an extent, it will be they who push you forward, they whot want you to be their boss, demand of you that you lead. You will be the Rules Player *par excellence*.

> LAUGH AT THEIR JOKES,
> BUT DON'T GO ON
> VACATION WITH THEM.

Know When to Break the Rules

Many excellent and committed Rules Players I meet start out following every Rule. When you're first setting out, this is a sensible approach. After all, the alternative is complacency and an assurance that "I can do this stuff," which certainly isn't true. None of us finds every situation effortless. It may be clear what we should do, but that doesn't always mean it's easy. And sometimes we're not sure which way to go.

So, by all means start out taking each Rule seriously. That's the general idea. However, as you become more comfortable and self-assured as a Rules Player and begin to develop sound instincts for Rules behavior, you can begin to loosen up. Many of the Rules will become automatic, and you'll no longer have to think about them. And once you reach this stage, you'll find that occasionally one of the Rules really isn't quite appropriate.

It's no good persuading yourself a Rule doesn't fit because you'd much rather not have to follow it. You need to be clear and objective. But when your instincts genuinely tell you to break a Rule, then go for it.

Personally, I find that there's rarely a need to break a Rule. I do break Rules occasionally. For example, a Rules Player never deliberately belittles other people in public, but about twice in my life I've encountered people who really needed to be belittled in public to stop them from doing it to others.

In the end it's about gut feeling. Follow the Rules until they're so ingrained they become instinct, and then trust your instincts. If you refer back to the Rules from time to time, and you work on the ones you find tricky, you can be confident that in time your instincts will serve you better than any book.